CARYL CHURCHILL

Caryl Churchill has written for the stage, television and radio. Her stage plays include *Owners* (Royal Court Theatre Upstairs, 1972); *Objections to Sex and Violence* (Royal Court, 1975), *Light Shining in Buckinghamshire* (Joint Stock on tour incl. Theatre Upstairs, 1976); *Vinegar Tom* (Monstrous Regiment on tour, incl. Half Moon and ICA, 1976); *Traps* (Theatre Upstairs , 1977); *Cloud Nine* (Joint Stock on tour incl. Royal Court, London, 1979, then Theatre de Lys, New York, 1981); *Three More Sleepless Nights* (Soho Poly and Theatre Upstairs, 1980); *Top Girls* (Royal Court London, then Public Theater, New York, 1982); *Fen* (Joint Stock on tour, incl. Almeida and Royal Court, London, then Public Theatre, New York, 1983); *Softcops* (RSC at the Pit, 1984); *A Mouthful of Birds* with David Lan (Joint Stock on tour, incl. Royal Court, 1986); *Serious Money* (Royal Court and Wyndham's, London, then Public Theater, New York, 1987); *Icecream* (Royal Court, 1989); *Mad Forest* (Central School of Speech and Drama, then Royal Court, 1990); *Lives of the Great Poisoners* with Orlando Gough and Ian Spink (Second Stride on tour, incl. Riverside Studios, London, 1991); *The Skriker* (Royal National Theatre, 1994); *Thyestes* translated from Seneca (Royal Court Theatre Upstairs, 1994); *Hotel* with Orlando Gough and Ian Spink (Second Stride on tour, incl. The Place, London, 1997); *This is a Chair* (London International Festival of Theatre at the Royal Court, 1997); *Blue Heart* (Joint Stock on tour, incl. Royal Court Theatre, 1997); *Far Away* (Royal Court Theatre Upstairs, 2000, and Albery, London, 2001, then New York Theatre Workshop, 2002); *A Number* (Royal Court Theatre Downstairs, 2002, then New York Theatre Workshop, 2004); *A Dream Play* after Strindberg (Royal National Theatre, 2005); *Drunk Enough to Say I Love You?* (Royal Court Theatre Upstairs, 2006, then Public Theater, New York, 2008); *Bliss*, translated from Olivier Choinière (Royal Court Theatre, 2008); *Seven Jewish Children – a play for Gaza* (Royal Court Theatre, 2009); *Love and Information* (Royal Court Theatre Downstairs, 2012); *Ding Dong the Wicked* (Royal Court Theatre Downstairs, 2012).

Other works by Caryl Churchill, published by Nick Hern Books

CARYL CHURCHILL

Plays: Four

introduced by the author

Hotel
This is a Chair
Blue Heart
Far Away
A Number
A Dream Play
(*translated from Strindberg*)
Drunk Enough to Say I Love You?

NICK HERN BOOKS

London

www.nickhernbooks.co.uk

A Nick Hern Book

Churchill Plays: Four first published in Great Britain as a paperback original in 2008 by Nick Hern Books Limited, The Glasshouse, 49a Goldhawk Road, London W12 8QP

Reprinted 2009 (twice), 2010, 2011, 2012, 2013, 2014

A Dream Play is based on a literal translation by Charlotte Barslund

Author photograph: Stephen Cummiskey
Cover design: Ned Hoste, 2H

Typeset by Country Setting, Kingsdown, Kent CT14 8ES
Printed in Great Britain by CPI Group (UK) Ltd

ISBN   978 1 85459 540 9

Contents

Introduction

Hotel, *This is a Chair* and the two plays in *Blue Heart* all come
from around the same time, 1994–5, and from a similar
mindset. *Hotel* isn't a play but an opera libretto. *This is a Chair*
is a series of impressive subjects that a play might address and
the scenes don't address them. *Heart's Desire* is a play that can't
happen, obsessively resetting itself back to the beginning every
time it veers off-course. *Blue Kettle* is a play infected with a virus.

Hotel was written for Orlando Gough, and Ian Spink directed it
for Second Stride with reckless generosity despite the large cast.
I fear the large company and few performances may have been
one of the reasons the Arts Council cut the grant of this great,
innovative company.

The first piece, itself originally called *Hotel*, was written first.
I've never liked too many words in an opera and don't want to
be reading while I listen or straining to extricate sentences from
the music. So I went for few words and no sentences, just
scraps of what the characters are thinking or saying, which can
easily be picked up and can also just be heard as sound when
they are repeated or combined. Occasionally people ask if it
can be performed as a play, without music, but that seems to
miss the point. The characters can sing together from their
separate rooms as they sit together on the same bed watching
the same TV.

We then decided to make a second piece, so we renamed *Hotel*
as *Eight Rooms* and the new piece *Two Nights*. Here the dancers
who played the silent couple in *Eight Rooms* played the central
characters, and Ian choreographed their hotel-room stories,
while the singers were more of a chorus. Their text is supposed
to be fragments of a diary found in the hotel room of someone
who has disappeared. I think it's all right to perform either of
the pieces separately.

Around this time I wrote a short scene of a quarrel, using just
scraps of what is said and racing through a whole evening in
five minutes. I can't remember if this was before or after I wrote
Hotel. I was looking at the same question – how little do we

need to hear to understand what's going on? – but from a different motive, not music but impatience. Soon after that I wrote *This is a Chair*, and later director Stephen Daldry and I decided to include the scene (as 'Hong Kong'), partly to make the play a bit longer, I think, and partly because it looked as if it would be fun to work on. It was, though it took a disproportionate amount of rehearsal: if time passes between every line, should the gestures and position of the actors change? And the scene has to go fast, of course, with no gaps for the missing time. The scene sits a little oddly in *This is a Chair* because it's written differently from the others but also I like it there, so it can be left in or out in performance. The titles should probably be updated for new productions, and I'm happy to have suggestions run by me. Nowadays 'The War in Afghanistan' would probably be a title, and 'Climate Change' would be there. Though not, of course, written about.

The *Blue Heart* plays, I realised afterwards, can be roughly linked in subject matter by being described as a family waiting for their daughter and a son looking for his mother. But the plays are McGuffins – my main intention was their destruction.

Some time after all this, 1999, I wrote *Far Away*, which feels to me quite different as the play isn't being undermined. The three parts can seem disconnected, linked only by the girl who goes through them and widening hostilities, but I think they are also linked by the characters' desire to be on the side of what's right.

A Number has cloning at the centre of its story but I never quite feel it's a play about cloning. The cloning's not quite a McGuffin but it does let me look at a lot of things that interest me. I realised after I'd written it that I'd thought about some of the same things in *Identical Twins* more than twenty-five years earlier. I'm reluctant to give advice rather than let the play stand on its own feet now, but I will point out that Michael isn't a fool. It's easy to make him a laughing stock to the audience, because he fails to come up with something that satisfies Salter, but his answers seem to me good ones and a serious answer to Salter's search for some essence of a person. That doesn't mean there aren't laughs in the scene.

I came up with a text of Strindberg's *Dream Play* for Katie Mitchell, who was planning to direct it at the National Theatre in London. I didn't go to the Swedish – which I don't know,

but looking at it would have told me something – but worked
from a translation by Charlotte Barslund, given to me by the
National. Katie had some cuts in mind and I made a few as
well. I slightly regret losing the first scene where the daughter
comes down to earth, which balances her departure at the end,
but apparently that was an afterthought of Strindberg's in any
case, and the focus of the production was not the daughter's
story but a dreamer's. There were more cuts in rehearsal, and
dance and more dreams, so this text isn't an account of the
production, but what I gave Katie as a starting point. I feel
wary of cuts and 'versions', as opposed to complete and skilful
translations by someone who knows both languages but
perhaps there's a place for both, for writers lucky enough to
still be performed when they're dead.

Drunk Enough to Say I Love You? was originally called in my head
'The Man Who Fell in Love with America'. But that seemed
to tell too much. A lot of people all over the world have a kind
of romance with America or its culture or the idea of it, even
if they also increasingly and simultaneously dislike it. Sam
was always Sam, as in Uncle, as in political cartoons where he
stands for America. The other character didn't have a name
while I was writing the play, and when I had to come up with
one I thought of Jack as an everyday name – Jack of all trades,
Jack the lad. What I didn't think, stupidly, was Union Jack,
which was the quite sensible conclusion some people jumped to.
That made the man in love with America be seen as Britain, as
Sam was America. It was hard enough anyway to understand
that Sam was a country while the person in love with him was
just a man, like someone in the audience, and now I'd shot
myself in the foot. I tried to get the play away from the mis-
conceptions for the New York production by changing the
man's name to Guy (a guy, ha ha, far too obvious but I was past
caring) and in Germany he was German. I'd always imagined
he would just be someone from whatever country the play was
done in. He could even be an American citizen in an American
production, patriotically in love with his country and increasingly
disillusioned. Another misconception was that the characters
stood for Bush and Blair, specially as they began to be port-
rayed in cartoons as lovers. But the play looks at America's
foreign policy from far further back, any time since the Second
World War. Some people seemed surprised by the Iraq War as
if it was an aberration caused by Bush and the neocons, but
though it's an extreme example it's not so different from the

general thrust of American policy for most of its history, and part of my point in writing the play was precisely that this was not just something that had come with Bush and would go away after him. I read a number of books to learn more details and found William Blum's *Rogue State* and *Killing Hope* particularly useful.

The love story is chronological and that is the story the actors play. The actions they are taking are divided into subjects – elections, bombing, trade – and in each scene they can be taken from any time but are happening now, in the moment, for the characters, who are fixing an election, bombing a country, as they speak. The problem of how to get in all those facts without being clunky, how to get the characters from one activity to the next, was solved, I hope, by using that same technique as in the little quarrel scene ten or so years earlier: moving swiftly on, giving just a few words and leaping forward to another part of the conversation. Again there's a problem of how to perform it, and the potential jerkiness of demonstrating the time gaps is probably too much for a longer piece. The challenge is for the emotional story between the lovers to stay continuous while the subject matter hurtles on and is a new moment in each line.

Caryl Churchill, 2008

HOTEL

Words
Caryl Churchill

Music
Orlando Gough

Direction/Choreography
Ian Spink

Introductions

CARYL CHURCHILL

Eight Rooms

I kept thinking about a lot of different stories all happening on
stage at once. How to cope with all those people talking at the
same time? Easily of course if they're not talking but singing,
and in any case I wanted to write an opera for Orlando. At
some point I had the idea of a hotel where we'd see all the
identical rooms superimposed as one room, all the people in
the same space. And what sort of words should they sing?
When I'm listening to sung words I like taking their meaning in
without any effort, and I'm also happy to hear them just as
sound. What I don't like is feeling I may be missing something
important if I don't follow every word. What do I want from
words in an opera? A situation, an emotion, an image. Some of
the sections that had stayed with me most from *Lives of the Great
Poisoners* (a 1991 piece with Orlando and Ian) had very simple
words that could be taken in quickly and repeated. The little
opera scene in *The Skriker* (1994, music by Judith Weir) had
words without the usual structure of sentences (welcome
homesick drink drank drunk) but it was easy to understand
what was happening. So in *Hotel*, how little need the characters
say to let us know enough about them? I decided there would
be no complete sentences, just little chunks of what was said or
thought, that could be absorbed first time round or in a repeat
or even never.

Two Nights

In *Eight Rooms* each of the thirteen singers is a different
character; in *Two Nights* they all sing a diary that has been left
in a hotel room. The silent performers in *Eight Rooms* now play
two people who spend different nights in the same room. We
want this piece to start from ideas about the choreography and
Ian maps out the two stories, though the first thing to be set is

the words, then the music, and the details of the choreography are to be worked out in rehearsal. Both the characters disappear in different ways, and the diary is written by someone who becomes invisible. What might be in a diary apart from how the body begins to vanish? Notes about other kinds of disappearance. On the internet I found worry about cities disappearing in smog, a magician making a building disappear, a Canadian legal judgement about objects that go missing, an anarchist using disappearance rather than confrontation as a 'logical radical option', and a spell for becoming invisible translated from Greek magical documents. Again I used few words, glimpses as we flick through someone else's diary.

ORLANDO GOUGH

Eight Rooms

Caryl says What do you like about opera? I say The bits when everyone sings at once.

So what about this? Caryl says: one night in a hotel; eight rooms are seen simultaneously. Excellent! Off we go.

People sing duets, trios, quartets with people they never meet. Their lives intersect in the realm of shared emotion, in the realm of counterpoint and polyphony.

The action is everyday, consciously undramatic.

Is it possible to write an opera of everyday life? Isn't there an inherent contradiction? Isn't the function of opera to deal with extremes of emotion? Should not action resolve character?

A fragmentary libretto. Already a move away from naturalism. Allows me to compose the music, i.e. make the text into music, rather than being dragged along by the words.

A cyclic structure. The piece ends almost as it began. A sense that the next night would be similar. We are interested in these people only while they are in the hotel. A crowd looked at from afar (with occasional help of a pair of binoculars).

Opera singers. NO!

Working with jazz singers. Should I give opportunities to improvise? Surely I am wasting their talent if I don't? However, I am not sure about this idea 'opportunities to improvise'. If the music after the improvised passage is not affected by the improvisation, then surely the improviser is just filling in time? . . . I get very excited by the idea of a completely improvised opera, and then funk it. Six months' rehearsal would be barely enough.

A lean, functional band: piano duet and double bass. Almost like a jazz rhythm section. A modest but utterly crucial role. However, the emotional energy must come from the singers. Thirteen singers and three players! – almost the mirror image of many modern chamber operas, where complex texture is created with an important role for the band and the singers are treated almost like instrumentalists.

Two Nights

A companion for *Eight Rooms* – not necessarily a friend. Same cast. What else happens in hotels? says Ian. A hotel is where you might go, for privacy, to do something lonely, radical, extreme, life changing, terminal. Sid Vicious.

I want the music to be very different from *Eight Rooms*: the singers will be a choir.

A diary has been left in the room. The singers will sing the contents of the diary.

A kind of song cycle. Harmony rather than counterpoint. (Yikes, not my strong point.) Drama! Risk! A linear structure – a sense of not being able to retrace one's steps. Though one might want to. A much darker piece than *Eight Rooms*.

The dancers, who have had a peripheral role in *Eight Rooms*, are now centre stage. The singers... sing, and occasionally take part in the action.

The subject matter of *Two Nights* is definitely 'operatic'. But we haven't written an opera...

Should the dancing mimic the text? NO! Should it ignore the text? Not quite – it should connect, but on an emotional rather than literal level.

The old problem again: the text and the music are written in advance; the choreography can't exist until rehearsals start. How can the choreographer be expected to work with such an unbending structure? We consider scrapping the text and the music and making a devised piece (on the same theme) in rehearsal. An exhilarating and alarming idea. The singers' ability to improvise is a catalyst. We funk it. Cowards! Two months' rehearsals needed, minimum.

'You put so much emotion into singing your love songs, spend the evening pouring your heart out, but then go back to your hotel alone.' k.d. lang (speaking in *The Independent*)

'To be inside that music, to be drawn into the circle of its repetitions: perhaps that is a place where one could finally disappear.' Paul Auster, *City of Glass* (Faber and Faber)

IAN SPINK

Eight Rooms

. . . began as a challenge. How do you fit fourteen hotel guests into one room? What happens when they all eventually go to bed? The potential for enormous traffic jams in such an intimate space seemed huge and fascinating. In rehearsal we were to discover that the simplest of acts, the cleaning of teeth, the hanging up of a dress, the reading of a magazine, demanded a relaxed yet rigorous precision when taking into account the thirteen other occupants of the space.

The hotel room channels many threads of action into a single stream of human experience covering a period of perhaps sixteen hours. Guests arrive, tiny incidents are briefly exposed; a drunken couple argue, a young woman dreams of a bird, an American plans a game of golf, a French couple drink tea, a business man rings home, two lovers whisper, a wife considers her marriage, a silent couple watch television. In one sense ordinary and unambiguous activities but collected together they produce a touching and mesmeric atmosphere. In the morning these people prepare to leave; a woman packs her case, a man comments on the weather, another orders breakfast, an insomniac finally succumbs to sleep. The sparse yet humane text combines with the music to produce a strangely uplifting piece of theatre.

Two Nights

Created some time later, *Two Nights* has become for me, an antidote to *Eight Rooms*. Here the challenge was, can you weave together three almost unrelated stories and play them out in the same location? The hotel room is now a more ambiguous, dangerous place, a catalyst for darker journeys, two of them danced, one of them sung to a sparkling counterpoint score. The singers have become a choral accompaniment and occasional extras to the choreographed action. A trapped woman struggles with her conscience and seeks salvation surrounded by strangers, a man haunted by his past is about to end his life. Their stories are danced out in extreme, dramatic bursts accompanied by entries from an abandoned diary, the diary of someone who has become invisible. The three self-contained threads playing simultaneously, are about magic, deception and transformation.

Hotel was first performed by Second Stride at the Schauspielhaus, Hanover, Germany, on 15 April 1997, and subsequently on tour, including to The Place, London, with the following cast:

Eight Rooms

TV/GHOST	Angela Elliott
SILENT WOMAN	Gabrielle McNaughton
SILENT MAN	Colin Poole
US WOMAN	Daniela Clynes
US MAN	Mick O'Connor
AFFAIR WOMAN	Jenny Miller
AFFAIR MAN	Richard Chew
OLD FRENCH WOMAN	Marjorie Keys
OLD FRENCH MAN	Andrew Bolton
GAY WOMAN (1)	G T Nash
GAY WOMAN (2)	Rebecca Askew
DRUNK WOMAN	Carol Grimes
DRUNK MAN	D W Matzdorf
BIRDBOOK WOMAN	Louise Field
BUSINESSMAN	Wayne Ellington

Two Nights

MAN	Colin Poole
WOMAN	Gabrielle McNaughton

A DIARY FOUND IN A HOTEL ROOM

Rebecca Askew, Andrew Bolton,
Richard Chew, Daniela Clynes,
Wayne Ellington, Angela Elliott,
Louise Field, Carol Grimes,
Marjorie Keys, D W Matzdorf,
Jenny Miller, G T Nash,
Mick O'Connor

Director/Choreographer Ian Spink
Music Orlando Gough
Designer Lucy Bevan

Acknowledgements

Quotes in the 'Will to Power' section from *TAZ* by Hakim Bay, published by Autonomedia

Quotes in the 'Spell' section from *Greek Magical Papyri including the Demotic Spells* by H. Dieter-Bitz, published by the University of Chicago Press © 1986, 1992

The musical score to *Hotel* by Orlando Gough is available for hire to amateur groups who wish to perform the play and have applied for a licence. Please apply to Nick Hern Books.

Eight Rooms

Characters

SILENT COUPLE
US COUPLE
AFFAIR COUPLE
OLD FRENCH COUPLE
GAY COUPLE
DRUNK COUPLE
BUSINESSMAN
BIRDBOOK WOMAN
TV
GHOST

Hotel bedroom. Large double bed, sink, wardrobe, TV.
It is eight identical hotel bedrooms superimposed. Each couple behaves as if they were alone in the room.

1. Arrivals

SILENT COUPLE *arrive, start to settle in.*
BUSINESSMAN *arrives, puts on TV, flops on bed.*

TV

rain later . . heavier and more prolonged
on to tomorrow

US COUPLE *arrive.*

US MAN

which is terrific. The window you get a view of the

US WOMAN

uh huh uh huh

AFFAIR WOMAN *arrives alone.*
OLD FRENCH COUPLE *arrive.*

OLD COUPLE

demain . . le fleuve . . en bateau . . si tu veux

GAY COUPLE *arrive.*

GAY 1

I told him

GAY 2

you tell him

AFFAIR MAN *arrives.*

AFFAIR MAN
Miss me?

AFFAIR WOMAN
Missed you. Miss me?

AFFAIR MAN
Missed you.

BIRDBOOK WOMAN *arrives. Starts to read hotel brochure.*

BIRDBOOK WOMAN
The hotel is situated . .
in every room . .
continental or full English
in case of fire.

OTHERS *join in brochure.*

2. **Settling In**

BUSINESSMAN *phones home.*

BUSINESSMAN
Hi darling . . no really . . yeh . . yeh . . put him on.
Hi darling . . you did? . . big kiss, bye bye.
Hi darling . . you did? . . big kiss, bye bye.
Darling . . bye bye . . big kiss, bye bye.

GAY 1
we don't have to

GAY 2
of course we don't

GAY 1
we can simply

GAY 2
spend some time

GAY 1
get to know each other

GAY 2
get to know each other?

GAY 1
again.

US MAN
Golf in the neighbourhood . .
little guy in reception made me laugh when he said . .
if we get an early night we can make an early . .

US WOMAN
uh huh uh huh uh huh

OLD COUPLE
son chapeau

They laugh.

AFFAIR COUPLE
can't believe
just so
nothing like
wonder

BIRDBOOK WOMAN *is reading a bird book.*

BIRDBOOK WOMAN
sparrowhawk . . tinted eggs . . sedges . . nightingale

DRUNK COUPLE *arrive cheerful and noisy.*

because I really sincerely do
you're completely right to
and he's such an arsehole
which nobody understands except you

3. TV

By now many people are lying on the bed watching TV, often changing channels.

TV

your mother's very upset . . further consultation . . returns to feed her young . . *in* London . .

VIEWERS

turn over turn over

BUSINESSMAN *reads a book.*

BUSINESSMAN

raced towards him . . headless . . blood on his

OLD WOMAN *reads a book.*

OLD WOMAN

longtemps soulagé. . son beau visage . .

4. Sleep

Most of them are in bed by now.

BIRDBOOK WOMAN *reads.*

BIRDBOOK WOMAN
Care charmer sleep son of the sable night . .
and let the day be time enough to mourn . .
and never wake to feel the day's disdain.

GAY COUPLE *and* AFFAIR COUPLE *quartet.*

your eyes
do you like?
this is so
my angel
skin
so wet
further and further
always

5. Quarrel

DRUNK COUPLE *quarrel loudly.*

what the hell do you think
shut up shut up
just say that again just
out get out
don't you dare
always knew
kill you
never

OTHERS *are alarmed by the noise.*

shall we phone the desk?
shall we bang on their door?
are they hurting each other?
shut the fuck up

*The drunk couple are exhausted, the quarrel ends, everyone settles down
again.*

TV

not quite far enough down the table
35 . . 42 . . 43 . .

TV is turned off.

6. Insomnia

Care charmer sleep continues.

INSOMNIAC (GAY 2)
I'm I'm afraid I'm afraid I I'm afraid I can't
I'm afraid I can't sleep
I'm afraid I can't sleep afraid I can't sleep
I can't sleep can't sleep sleep

7. Obsessive

US MAN *gets up quietly. All is quiet except insomniac.*

He does ritual movements. He keeps stopping and going back to the beginning.

US WOMAN *wakes up.*

US WOMAN
What?

US MAN
Honey.

US WOMAN
What you doing?

US MAN
Honey.

US WOMAN
Come to bed.

US MAN
Honey.

He goes back to bed, seems to sleep.

8. Lonely

US WOMAN

hold you close because I'm lonely
are you there? because I'm lonely
when I hold you close it makes me lonely
never close never there
lonely

GAY 2 *has been continuing insomniac song. Now sings with* US
WOMAN.

afraid and lonely
can't sleep and lonely
hold you close because I'm lonely
I wish I was with
afraid I can't sleep
lonely

9. Anguish

AFFAIR WOMAN *wakes up.*

AFFAIR WOMAN
afraid I can't sleep
how I miss
what if I lose
danger danger
children in danger
gone what if they're gone what if

AFFAIR MAN *wakes and soothes her.*

hush hush hush

10. Dreams

GAY 1 *is dreaming*

walking down the road I saw a
car who is a man who is a
flying down the hill I saw a
bird who is a meeting of the
doctors of the house who is a
cupboard with a cat who is a
mother of a yellow and a
running up the mountain
to get before it happens
to the child who is a
bird who is a falling

OLD FRENCH MAN *is dreaming*

l'oiseau blanc dans le metro
le chapeau dans le bateau

BIRDBOOK WOMAN *is dreaming*

up
round
down
in

INSOMNIAC GAY *continues during this.*

11. Obsessive 2

US MAN *gets up again while dreaming is going on, starts rituals as before.*

BUSINESSMAN *dreams.*

a cat who is a
woman with a furry and a
purring and a further and
further and a further and a
fury and a

US MAN *finishes rituals satisfactorily and goes back to bed.*

Silence. Everyone is still.

12. Ghost

GHOST

It's me.
Let me into your sleep.
Let me in when you wake.
I've been dead so long
I've forgotten why
I've not gone away.

I walk out of the night
can't you hear
can't you see
it's me
I've forgotten who
I've forgotten why.

13. Dawn

Silence. But now and then a little sound from the insomniac.

OLD FRENCH WOMAN *wakes.*

OLD WOMAN
tous les matins
très bonne heure
j'ai peur de mourir
les oiseaux
j'ai peur

BIRDBOOK WOMAN *wakes.*

BIRDBOOK WOMAN
blackbird thrush starling wren

INSOMNIAC *falls asleep.*

OLD WOMAN *gets up.*

OLD WOMAN
je me lave
très bonne heure
j'n'ai plus peur
le matin
les oiseaux

14. Morning

BIRDBOOK WOMAN *gets up and dresses, takes birdbook and binoculars and goes out.*

BIRDBOOK WOMAN
blackbird

OLD WOMAN *makes tea and wakes* OLD MAN.

AFFAIR COUPLE *reprise 'your eyes' and goodbye goodbye.*

GAY 1 *wakes.* GAY 2, INSOMNIAC, *still sleeping.*

GAY 1
don't know what you want
but I want you
again

US MAN *wakes cheerful,* US WOMAN *still sleepy.*

US MAN
looks like a great day

US WOMAN
uh huh

US MAN
not a cloud in the sky

US WOMAN
uh huh

BUSINESSMAN *puts on TV.*

TV
after the break . . relationships expert . .

BUSINESSMAN *phones home.*

Hi darling . . big kiss

SILENT COUPLE *who have been asleep throughout wake up.*

DRUNK COUPLE *waking up.*

my head bang my belly bang my eyes bang my knees bang my
heart bang

OLD COUPLE
on va au fleuve
allons vite

OLD COUPLE *leave.*

AFFAIR WOMAN *leaves.*

AFFAIR MAN
your eyes
my angel
what if I lose

This becomes duet with GAY 1.
INSOMNIAC *still asleep.*
AFFAIR MAN *leaves.*

BUSINESSMAN
bacon and eggs and tomato and sausage and mushroom
and bacon

GAY 1 *joins in.*

BUSINESSMAN *leaves for breakfast.*

GAY 1 *can't wake* INSOMNIAC *so leaves for breakfast too.*

DRUNK COUPLE *manage to leave.*

SILENT COUPLE *leave.*

Nobody left but INSOMNIAC *asleep.*

The TV is still on.

TV
bright spells and scattered
clearing later
shaping up to be a nice
and over now to

Two Nights

From a diary found in a hotel room

Hand Gone

my hand has gone
january
very late at night
today my whole left side
six and a half minutes
disappeared

July

july
city out of sight in the haze
wish I could disappear
magician made the tower disappear from the ground up
and all the people who lived

Thin

thin and cold
the wind blows right through me

Mysterious Disappearance

mysterious disappearance

the judge said
any disappearance or loss
unknown puzzling baffling
hard to explain or understand
mysterious disappearance

a ring left on a dresser
later it's not there
no evidence of theft
the loss would be mysterious disappearance

Suddenly

suddenly at a party
ran out invisible and hid
saw myself slowly appear in the mirror on the wall in the
sauntered downstairs for a drink
'where have you been?'

try to stop fading but

or shall I try to disappear?

no good the way I am

Will to Power

the will to power as disappearance
it says
logical radical option for our time
it says
not a disaster not a death
but a way to what?

Shadow

will I still have a shadow?
will I still have a mind?
wind blow through
will invisible eyes still see?

Spell

the spell if I dare
here in a hotel room
eye of a nightowl
smear your whole body
say to Helios
by your great name
Zizia
Lailam
a a a a
I I I I
o o o o
ieo
in the presence of any man until sunset
make me invisible

Hand . . Light

held my hand up to the light and

THIS IS A CHAIR

This is a Chair was first performed by the Royal Court Theatre at the Duke of York's Theatre, London, on 25 June 1997, with the following cast:

JULIAN	Linus Roache
MARY	Amanda Plummer
FATHER	Marion Bailey
MURIEL	Harriet Spencer
TED	Euan Bremner
ANN	Diane Parish
JOHN	Lennie James
DEIRDRE	Liz Smith
POLLY	Helen McCarthy
TOM	Desmond Barrit
LEO	Timothy Spall
CHARLIE	Andy Serkis
MADDY	Cecilia Noble
ERIC	Ray Winstone

Director Stephen Daldry
Designer Ian MacNeil
Lighting Designer Lizz Poulter

Characters

JULIAN
MARY

FATHER
MOTHER
MURIEL
TED
ANN
JOHN
DEIRDRE
POLLY
TOM
LEO
CHARLIE
ERIC
MADDY

**The title of each scene must be clearly displayed
or announced.**

The War in Bosnia

JULIAN *is waiting in a London street holding a bunch of flowers.*

MARY *arrives.*

MARY   I'm so sorry.

JULIAN   That's all right, don't worry.

MARY   Have you been here ages?

JULIAN   I got you these.

MARY   They're beautiful.

JULIAN   I don't know what you like.

MARY   Thank you very much.

JULIAN   I like orange and blue together, I don't know
            if you do, I thought of roses but I think roses
            are a bit dull, I don't like pink and red very
            much as colours, I don't mind yellow but I
            thought these.

MARY   Listen, I'm afraid there's a problem.

JULIAN   Yes.

MARY   I've made a stupid mistake.

JULIAN   Never mind.

MARY   No but I've made two different arrangements
            for the same evening, I've doublebooked
            myself, I don't know how I can be so stupid.

JULIAN   So you have to make a phonecall or . . . ?

MARY   No, it's really awful, what I have to do is
            jump in a cab and go whizzing off. Because I
            have to be there by half past seven.

JULIAN   Something starts at half past seven?

MARY   Yes and I couldn't reach the other person
            and anyway the tickets and . . .

JULIAN   Don't worry.

MARY   It is a concert I particularly . . .

JULIAN   Yes of course. We'd better look for a cab.

MARY   It was the arrangement I made first you see
            and somehow it slipped my mind and I
            thought we might have time for a drink
            anyway but then I was late finishing work
            and there was a hold-up on the tube it
            stopped in the tunnel for about five minutes
            people were starting to get nervous you could
            see from the way they kept on reading or just
            staring into space but deliberately because
            they were getting nervous and anyway can
            we make it another time I'm really sorry.

JULIAN   Don't worry.

MARY   What about Tuesday?

JULIAN   I can't do Tuesdays.

MARY   Or Thursday, no wait I can't do Thursday,
            Friday oh shit, the week after, any night you
            like, not Wednesday.

JULIAN   Thursday then.

MARY   Thursday week then.

JULIAN   Same time same place?

MARY   Yes this is good for me. I won't be late.

JULIAN   Don't worry. There's a cab.

MARY   I'm really sorry.

JULIAN   Byebye.

Pornography and Censorship

FATHER, MOTHER *and* MURIEL *at dinner.*

FATHER   Is Muriel going to eat her dinner?

MOTHER   Yes, eat up, Muriel.

FATHER   Have a special bite of daddy's.

MOTHER   Yes, eat up, Muriel.

FATHER   Muriel, if you don't eat your dinner you
              know what's going to happen to you.

MOTHER   Yes, eat up, Muriel.

The Labour Party's Slide to the Right

TED *and* ANN *in Ann and her boyfriend's third-floor flat.*

TED   I don't believe it.

ANN   You did that.

TED   John, John get in here quick.

ANN   You did that coming in here.

               JOHN *comes in.*

JOHN   I can't find nothing in the bedroom.

TED   John you won't believe this.

JOHN   Where is he?

ANN   It's your fault coming in here.

TED   He ran on the balcony and jumped over.

JOHN   He what?

TED   I can't look.

ANN   I'm going down. You did it, I'll tell everyone you did it, why can't you keep out of my life.

               ANN *goes.*

TED   I just said we've had enough of you. I didn't touch him.

JOHN   He knew what we was here for.

TED   He knew we were here to say you got our sister on drugs.

JOHN	And we said that.
TED	That's all we said.
JOHN	We weren't going to kill him or nothing.
TED	We were going to give him a smack.
JOHN	That's all right. Anyone expects a smack.
TED	We'll say exactly what happened. We don't need a story, do we, I mean what happened is what happened is perfectly all right.
JOHN	He might not be dead you know.
TED	I can't look.
JOHN	I'll look.
TED	Go on then.
JOHN	Yes I'm going to.
TED	He must have been out of his head is what it is.
JOHN	They'll see what he was on at the hospital.
TED	Maybe it's something he was going to do whether we come or not.
JOHN	Don't be stupid.
TED	So are you going to look or what?
JOHN	Yes I'm going to look.
TED	What a stupid bastard.
JOHN	Do you think she's down there by now? I'll have a look.

Animal Conservation and Third World Economies: the Ivory Trade

DEIRDRE *and* POLLY.

DEIRDRE	I'm going to hospital on Monday.
POLLY	Nothing serious?
DEIRDRE	No not at all but I've got to swallow a tube.
POLLY	I could go with you if you like.
DEIRDRE	No, it's nothing, I've done it before. You can do it with drugs or without.
POLLY	With.
DEIRDRE	I did do with the first time, I wasn't given a choice, but last time they said it only takes a couple of minutes do you want to try without. I said how often do people do that and they said about fifty fifty and I said and what do they say about it afterwards and they said oh they're fine about it, honestly, but of course if you haven't anything to do this afternoon and don't mind being drugged up − so put like that of course it was a challenge.
POLLY	And was it horrible?
DEIRDRE	The worst bit's when it goes over the throat. You have to keep breathing deeply, like being in labour except not. But everything taking second place to your body. And when it's over you feel terrific. I walked home because I'd got a whole extra afternoon but that was

stupid because I got exhausted because I
hadn't eaten or drunk anything since half
past seven. And of course at the time I
thought it was good not putting poison in my
body but afterwards I thought they were just
trying to save money.

POLLY   Of course they were. Didn't you realise that?

DEIRDRE   So maybe on Monday I'll have the drugs.

POLLY   I'd definitely have the drugs.

DEIRDRE   I probably will. Yes I think I'll definitely go
             for the drugs.

Hong Kong

TOM *and* LEO.

TOM	How could you do that you lied to me yes no I don't want to hear
LEO	very funny I don't care I don't care what you
TOM	just about enough
LEO	and I suppose you never?
TOM	why don't we just why don't we just now wait a minute
LEO	can't stand it can't
TOM	get this sorted out. Why in particular?
LEO	no good coming in now and saying
TOM	but listen why don't we just
LEO	too late
TOM	impossible to talk to
LEO	should have thought of that
TOM	you are so
LEO	piss off.
TOM	Not the first time
LEO	can't trust you with the simplest
TOM	no point in even

LEO	for instance and then last week you
TOM	how could you do that
LEO	and what you said was you wouldn't dream
TOM	and it doesn't even stand up I'd have to be stupid
LEO	stupid stupid stupid
TOM	break your neck
LEO	and you smell bad
TOM	if you could see yourself
LEO	piggy eyes piggy eyes piggy eyes
TOM	don't just don't even start don't just I'm warning you now don't
LEO	never did anyway
TOM	what the fuck you
LEO	on Wednesday at half past eleven when we'd specifically
TOM	two hundred pounds I don't understand how you can
LEO	because that's where you were don't bother denying it
TOM	and then you blame me
LEO	because I saw her in Safeways and she
TOM	don't let me see him again that's all or I'll
LEO	in our own bed
TOM	no.
LEO	I'm going to

TOM	fine by me
LEO	because I never
TOM	don't fancy you any more have to imagine
LEO	every time you come into the house my heart
TOM	haven't ever liked you
LEO	disgust me.

Their friend CHARLIE *arrives.*

TOM	well well well well well
LEO	long time
TOM	wet coat
CHARLIE	ah lovely
TOM	how you
CHARLIE	traffic
TOM	pretty busy
CHARLIE	seen old Joey lately because I've
LEO	house in the south of France
CHARLIE	running all over town trying to
TOM	rollmop herrings
CHARLIE	must have been terrible for you
LEO	and you've heard about Rose and
TOM	so we put in an offer of twenty thousand less than
CHARLIE	halfway to America by now.
LEO	So how's Wendy are you still
CHARLIE	terrible headaches

TOM   always remember that summer when

CHARLIE   the train to Brindisi

LEO   and the smell of the rain on the dust

CHARLIE   I do of course understand her point of view
               I wouldn't want to

TOM   always was a bit

LEO   emphasis on personal development

CHARLIE   her mother screeching positively screeching I
               couldn't

TOM   a good acupuncturist

LEO   up at half past five in the summer when the
               light

CHARLIE   my cousin in Australia

TOM   on the other hand

LEO   yes I wouldn't want to

CHARLIE   helps to talk things over with

TOM   not getting any younger

CHARLIE   don't know what to think

LEO   and is it this weekend we put the clocks back
               or is it back I never I have to work it out on
               my fingers same with America if I

TOM   stay to supper?

CHARLIE   my aunt's cat it got hit by a car and I said I'd

LEO   onion soup

CHARLIE   you are the loveliest

LEO   if you want to go to a movie, I haven't seen

TOM   supposed to be terrifying

CHARLIE   though I didn't think so much of his

LEO   the bit where they fell down the stairs and
                 the

CHARLIE   so I'll call you next week and maybe we can

LEO   that would be lovely

TOM   great to see you

LEO   give my love to

CHARLIE   sorry I'm a bit

LEO   next week.

                 CHARLIE *goes.*

                 putting on weight

TOM   having rather a difficult

LEO   work's not what it was of course but he didn't

TOM   why don't we just get a curry in I really fancy
                 a

LEO   so tired I could

TOM   hot bath

LEO   hey

TOM   yes well

LEO   exhausted

TOM   quarrelling is so

LEO   oh god

TOM   come here and let me

LEO   you don't really

TOM   let me just

LEO   because I do still

TOM   you're such a

LEO   not all my

TOM   don't start

LEO   love it when you

The Northern Ireland Peace Process

FATHER, MOTHER *and* MURIEL *at dinner.*

FATHER   Is Muriel going to eat her dinner?

MOTHER   Yes, eat up, Muriel.

FATHER   Have a special bite of daddy's.

MOTHER   Yes, eat up, Muriel.

FATHER   Muriel, if you don't eat your dinner you
              know what's going to happen to you.

MOTHER   Yes, eat up, Muriel.

Genetic Engineering

ERIC *and* MADDY *on their way to bed.*

MADDY	What was that? was that a bomb but far more likely
ERIC	no far more likely
MADDY	more likely a building some kind of construction
ERIC	demolition
MADDY	some kind of building
ERIC	some kind of building site or a road accident a crash but it's the wrong kind of sound for that it was more
MADDY	what, more
ERIC	more whoosh in it not so much metal
MADDY	like a firework can be like that like a rocket
ERIC	yes but no it was bigger
MADDY	no but they can those public ones set off huge
ERIC	so anyway I don't think it was a bomb anyway
MADDY	no I never thought it was a bomb. We could notice what time it is just to
ERIC	yes because you remember that time

MADDY	yes we said what was that but we didn't think anything of it
ERIC	no I did think
MADDY	and later it had been ten past one and we said
ERIC	yes you said that must be what we heard because we'd just sat down to the soup
MADDY	yes we said we must have heard it because it was ten past one.
ERIC	Well it's near enough half past eleven.
MADDY	I'm going to bed.
ERIC	Go on then, I'm coming.
MADDY	Yes but do come. You'll sit.
ERIC	No I am coming.
MADDY	I'm not sure I'm sleepy anyway.
ERIC	I'm not going to have a bath I had a bath yesterday I don't feel like a bath.
MADDY	No don't have a bath have one in the morning.

**The Impact of Capitalism on the
Former Soviet Union**

End.

BLUE HEART

Blue Heart was first produced by Out of Joint and the Royal
Court Theatre at the Theatre Royal, Bury St Edmunds, on
14 August 1997. It was first performed at the Traverse Theatre,
Edinburgh, on 19 August 1997 and opened at the Royal Court
Theatre, London, on 17 September 1997, with the following
cast:

Heart's Desire	*Blue Kettle*	
	MOTHER	Gabrielle Blunt
SUZY	ENID	Jacqueline Defferary
YOUNG WOMAN		Karina Fernandez
BRIAN	MR VANE	Bernard Gallagher
ALICE	MRS PLANT	Valerie Lilley
MAISIE	MRS OLIVER	Mary Macleod
	MRS VANE	Eve Pearce
LEWIS	DEREK	Jason Watkins
	MISS CLARENCE	Anna Wing
CHILDREN		Played by local children

Director Max Stafford-Clark
Designer Julian McGowan
Lighting Designer Johanna Town
Sound Designer Paul Arditti

The same production was revived for an international tour
in 1998, with the following cast changes:

Heart's Desire	*Blue Heart*	
SUZY	ENID	Sally Rogers
YOUNG WOMAN		Kirsty Bushell
BRIAN	MR VANE	Ewan Hooper
	MRS VANE	Doreen Mantle
LEWIS	DEREK	Pearce Quigley

The production received its American premiere at the Brooklyn
Academy of Music, New York, on 27 Jan 1999, with the same
cast.

Heart's Desire

Characters

BRIAN

ALICE

MAISIE

SUSY

LEWIS

LOTS OF CHILDREN

TWO GUNMEN

YOUNG AUSTRALIAN WOMAN

OFFICIAL

BIRD

Brian and Alice are married. Maisie is Brian's sister. They are all about 60. Susy, their daughter, is 35, Lewis, their son, is younger.

The scene is Brian and Alice's kitchen.

ALICE and MAISIE. ALICE *setting knives and forks on table,* MAISIE *fidgets about the room.* BRIAN *enters putting on a red sweater.*

BRIAN   She's taking her time.

ALICE   Not really.

They all stop, BRIAN *goes out. Others reset to beginning and do exactly what they did before as* BRIAN *enters putting on a tweed jacket.*

BRIAN   She's taking her time.

ALICE   Not really.

They all stop, BRIAN *goes out, others reset and* BRIAN *enters putting on an old cardigan.*

BRIAN   She's taking her time.

ALICE   Not really.

BRIAN   We should have met the plane.

ALICE   We should not.

MAISIE   What I really envy her for is the fauna
            because it's down a completely separate
            branch of evolution and I would love I would
            really love to see a platypus, not in a zoo but
            in its natural habitat. Imagine going to feed
            the ducks and there is something that is not a
            duck and nor is it a waterrat or a mole, it's
            the paws make me think of a mole, but
            imagine this furry creature with its ducky
            face, it makes you think what else could have
            existed, tigers with trunks, anyway the
            platypus has always been my favourite

animal, it doesn't lay eggs like a duck, it's a
marsupial like a kangaroo so the baby's born
like a thread like a speck and has to crawl
into the pouch, is that right, is a platypus a
marsupial or not actually I'm not sure about
that, maybe it does lay eggs like a duck, I'll
look it up or I'll ask her when she comes and
I wonder if she's ever seen one, maybe she
went swimming in a river and there was this
little furry –

Reset to top. BRIAN *comes in putting on old
cardigan.*

BRIAN   She's taking her time.

ALICE   Not really.

BRIAN   We should have met the plane.

ALICE   We should not.

BRIAN   She'll be exhausted.

ALICE   She's a woman of thirtyfive.

BRIAN   How can you speak of your daughter?

ALICE   She's a woman of thirtyfive.

BRIAN   You're so right of course.

ALICE   She can travel round the world, she can
            travel the last few miles.

BRIAN   It's so delightful for you always being so right.

ALICE   That's it.

BRIAN   It's what?

ALICE   I'm leaving.

BRIAN   Oh ha ha we're all supposed to be frantic
            and beg you to stay and say very sorry.

ALICE	I wouldn't bother.
BRIAN	I'm not going to bother don't worry.
	Exit ALICE.
MAISIE	Alice?
	BRIAN *and* MAISIE *wait.*
BRIAN	She'll just have a cry.
	ALICE *enters in coat with bag.*
ALICE	Tell her I'm sorry and I'll phone later to tell her where I am.
	Exit ALICE.
BRIAN	Was that the front door? Alice? Alice.
MAISIE	I don't think you –
	Reset to top, ALICE *in room as before,* MAISIE *as before,* BRIAN *enters putting on old cardigan.*
BRIAN	She's taking her time.
ALICE	Not really.
BRIAN	We should have met the plane.
ALICE	We should not.
BRIAN	She'll be exhausted.
ALICE	She's a woman of thirtyfive.
BRIAN	How can you speak of your daughter?
ALICE	She's a woman of thirtyfive.
BRIAN	You're so right of course.
ALICE	She can travel round the world, she can travel the last few miles.

BRIAN	It's so delightful for you always being so right.
ALICE	She didn't want to be met.
MAISIE	She'll be here in a few minutes.
BRIAN	I'm talking about spontaneity
ALICE	She doesn't want fuss.
BRIAN	She says that but it wouldn't be if she didn't know she was being met and there we just were or there I was –

Phone rings.

Hello? speaking. Ah. Right. Yes. Thank you.

MAISIE	What?
BRIAN	There's been an accident.
ALICE	The plane?
BRIAN	The tube. Didn't I say we should have met her?
ALICE	Is she – ?

Set back to top as before. BRIAN *enters putting on old cardigan.*

BRIAN	She's taking her time.
ALICE	Not really.
BRIAN	We should have met the plane.
ALICE	We should not.
BRIAN	She'll be exhausted.
ALICE	She's a woman of thirtyfive.
BRIAN	How can you speak of your daughter?
ALICE	She's a woman of thirtyfive.

BRIAN	You're so right of course.
ALICE	She can travel round the world, she can travel the last few miles.
BRIAN	It's so delightful for you always being so right.
ALICE	She didn't want to be met.
MAISIE	She'll be here in a few minutes.
BRIAN	I'm talking about spontaneity
ALICE	She doesn't want fuss.
BRIAN	She says that but it wouldn't be if she didn't know she was being met and there we just were or there I was if you insisted on not coming, she'd like it when it happened, the moment she caught sight she'd be delighted.
ALICE	Well we didn't so I don't see the point of worrying about it now.
BRIAN	She'll never come home from Australia again.
ALICE	What do you mean?
	MAISIE *trips over.*
	Oh, what?
BRIAN	What the hell?
MAISIE	Sorry, all right, I'm all right.
ALICE	You haven't hurt yourself?
MAISIE	No. Yes. Not really.
ALICE	Can you get up?
MAISIE	Yes of course. Well. It's just my ankle. Oh dear.

BRIAN	How did you do that?
ALICE	Sit down and let's have a look at it.
MAISIE	Oh ow. No no it's nothing. Ow.

Set back. BRIAN *enters putting on cardigan.*

BRIAN	She's taking her time.
ALICE	Not really.
BRIAN	We should have met the plane.
ALICE	We should not.
BRIAN	She'll be exhausted.
ALICE	She's a woman of thirtyfive.
BRIAN	How can you speak of your daughter.
ALICE	She's a woman of thirtyfive.
BRIAN	You're so right of course.
ALICE	She can travel round the world, she can travel the last few miles.
BRIAN	It's so delightful for you always being so right.
ALICE	She didn't want to be met.
MAISIE	She'll be here in a few minutes.
BRIAN	I'm talking about spontaneity.
ALICE	She doesn't want fuss.
BRIAN	She says that but it wouldn't be if she didn't know she was being met and there we just were or there I was if you insisted on not coming, she'd like it when it happened, the moment she caught sight she'd be delighted.
ALICE	Well we didn't so I don't see the point of worrying about it now.

BRIAN	She'll never come home from Australia again.
ALICE	What do you mean? of course she'll come again.
BRIAN	In the event she goes back of course she'll come again but she'll never come back for the first time again.

Enter LEWIS, *drunk.*

LEWIS	Where is she?
BRIAN	You're not coming in here in that condition.
LEWIS	Where's my big sister? I want to give her a kiss.
BRIAN	You'll see her when you're sober.
ALICE	Now it's all right, Brian. Susy isn't here yet, Lewis.
LEWIS	You've probably got her hidden under the table. Dad knows where she is, don't you Dad? Daddy always knows where Susy is. Hello Aunty Maisie, want a drink? Let's go to the pub, Maisie, and get away from this load of –

LEWIS *goes, setback as before. This time do the repeat at double speed, all movements accurate though fast.*

BRIAN	She's taking her time.
ALICE	Not really.
BRIAN	We should have met the plane.
ALICE	We should not.
BRIAN	She'll be exhausted.
ALICE	She's a woman of thirtyfive.

BRIAN	How can you speak of your daughter?
ALICE	She's a woman of thirtyfive.
BRIAN	You're so right of course.
ALICE	She can travel round the world, she can travel the last few miles.
BRIAN	It's so delightful for you always being so right.
ALICE	She didn't want to be met.
MAISIE	She'll be here in a few minutes.
BRIAN	I'm talking about spontaneity.
ALICE	She doesn't want fuss.
BRIAN	She says that but it wouldn't be if she didn't know she was being met and there we just were or there I was if you insisted on not coming, she'd like it when it happened, the moment she caught sight she'd be delighted.
ALICE	Well we didn't so I don't see the point of worrying about it now.
BRIAN	She'll never come home from Australia again.
ALICE	What do you mean? of course she'll come again.
BRIAN	In the event she goes back of course she'll come again but she'll never come back for the first time again.
	Resume normal speed.
MAISIE	It's all this waiting.
ALICE	I hope she does come soon because I'm getting hungry.
BRIAN	You don't have to wait to eat.

ALICE   No it's her special lunch.

MAISIE   Are you going to tell her straight away?

BRIAN   That's not something for you to worry about,
               Maisie.

ALICE   We're all in it together.

MAISIE   We've all got perfectly good alibis.

BRIAN   But they don't believe alibis any more. It's all
               forensic, it's all genetic.

ALICE   But there can't be any forensic if none of us
               did anything, I don't know why you have to
               act like a guilty person when it's nothing to
               do with any of us except that the body was
               found in our garden, it was dumped in our
               garden as everybody knows.

MAISIE   I keep telling the police about the postman
               but they haven't taken it in.

BRIAN   I happen to know that a great many people
               are wrongfully convicted and I don't live in a
               dream that suggests that terrible things only
               befall people in newspapers.

MAISIE   So I'll just say nothing and leave it to you.

               Reset to just after 'all this waiting'.

ALICE   I hope she does come soon because I'm
               getting hungry.

BRIAN   You don't have to wait to eat.

ALICE   No it's her special lunch.

BRIAN   I should just go ahead and eat since you've
               clearly no sense of occasion anyway. She's
               not going to care if there's lunch, she'll be
               exhausted, she'll go to bed.

ALICE   That's all right if that's what she wants to do.

BRIAN   You make yourself a doormat to that girl,
               you always did, she won't be grateful for
               lunch she'll be on a diet.

MAISIE   Now the one diet that is a good diet is
               the Hay diet which is to do with not
               combining –   ˙

               Reset to just after 'wants to do'.

BRIAN   You make yourself a doormat to that girl,
               you always did, she won't be grateful for
               lunch she'll be on a diet.

ALICE   Are you pleased she's coming back?

BRIAN   What's the matter with you now?

ALICE   You don't sleem peased – you don't pleem
               seased –

               Reset to after 'coming back'.

BRIAN   What's the matter with you now?

ALICE   You don't seem pleased, you seem cross.

MAISIE   The tube's very quick, she'll be here in no
               time I'm sure.

               *A horde of small children rush in, round the room
               and out again.*

               Reset to after 'of course she'll come again'.

BRIAN   In the event she goes back of course she'll
               come again but she'll never come back for
               the first time again.

MAISIE   It's all this waiting.

ALICE   I hope she does come soon because I'm
               getting hungry.

BRIAN	You don't have to wait to eat.
ALICE	No it's her special lunch.
BRIAN	I should just go ahead and eat since you've clearly no sense of occasion anyway. She's not going to care if there's lunch, she'll be exhausted, she'll go to bed.
ALICE	That's all right if that's what she wants to do.
BRIAN	You make yourself a doormat to that girl, you always did, she won't be grateful for lunch she'll be on a diet.
ALICE	Are you pleased she's coming back?
BRIAN	What's the matter with you now?
ALICE	You don't seem pleased, you seem cross.
MAISIE	The tube's very quick, she'll be here in no time I'm sure.
BRIAN	You're the thing makes me cross, drive me insane with your wittering.
ALICE	This should be a lovely day. You spoil everything.
BRIAN	You've done it now, it was a lovely day, you've spoilt it.

Enter LEWIS, *drunk.*

LEWIS	I'm unhappy. What are you going to do about it?
ALICE	You know you have to help yourself, Lewis.
LEWIS	But it never stops.
BRIAN	Lewis, I wish you'd died at birth. If I'd known what you'd grow up like I'd have killed either you or myself the day you were born.

LEWIS   You see this is where I get it from. Is it any wonder?

Reset to after 'doesn't want fuss'.

BRIAN   She says that but it wouldn't be if she didn't know she was being met and there we just were or there I was if you insisted on not coming, she'd like it when it happened, the moment she caught sight she'd be delighted.

ALICE   Well we didn't so I don't see the point of worrying about it now.

BRIAN   She'll never come home from Australia again.

ALICE   What do you mean? of course she'll come again.

BRIAN   In the event she goes back of course she'll come again but she'll never come back for the first time again.

MAISIE   It's all this waiting.

ALICE   I hope she does come soon because I'm getting hungry.

BRIAN   You don't have to wait to eat.

ALICE   No it's her special lunch.

BRIAN   I should just go ahead and eat since you've clearly no sense of occasion anyway. She's not going to care if there's lunch, she'll be exhausted, she'll go to bed.

ALICE   That's all right if that's what she wants to do.

BRIAN   You make yourself a doormat to that girl, you always did, she won't be grateful for lunch she'll be on a diet.

ALICE   Are you pleased she's coming back?

BRIAN	What's the matter with you now?
ALICE	You don't seem pleased, you seem cross.
MAISIE	The tube's very quick, she'll be here in no time I'm sure.
BRIAN	You're the thing makes me cross, drive me insane with your wittering.
ALICE	This should be a lovely day. You spoil everything.
BRIAN	You've done it now, it was a lovely day, you've spoilt it.
ALICE	All I'm saying is be nice to her.
BRIAN	Be nice to her?
ALICE	Yes I'm just saying be nice to her.

Two GUNMEN *burst in and kill them all, then leave.*

Reset to top. As far as possible keep the movements that go with the part lines.

BRIAN	She's taking
ALICE	Not
BRIAN	We should have
ALICE	We should not
BRIAN	She'll be
ALICE	She's a woman
BRIAN	How can you speak
ALICE	She's a
BRIAN	You're so
ALICE	She can travel

BRIAN	It's so delightful
ALICE	She didn't want
MAISIE	She'll be here
BRIAN	I'm talking about
ALICE	She doesn't
BRIAN	She says that but
ALICE	Well we didn't
BRIAN	She'll never
ALICE	What do you
BRIAN	In the event
MAISIE	It's all this
ALICE	I hope she
BRIAN	You don't have to
ALICE	No it's
BRIAN	I should just
ALICE	That's all right if
BRIAN	You make yourself a
ALICE	Are you pleased
BRIAN	What's the matter
ALICE	You don't seem
MAISIE	The tube's very
BRIAN	You're the thing
ALICE	This should be a lovely
BRIAN	You've done it

ALICE	All I'm saying is
BRIAN	Be nice
ALICE	Yes I'm just saying be nice to her.
BRIAN	When am I not nice to her? am I not a good father is that what you're going to say? do you want to say that? say it.
ALICE	I'm just –
BRIAN	Say it say it.
ALICE	Just be nice to her that's all.
BRIAN	Nice.
ALICE	Fine, you're going to be nice that's all I'm saying.
BRIAN	I should leave you. I'm the one should have gone to Australia.
ALICE	I wish you had.
BRIAN	Snipsnap, sharp tongue.
ALICE	No I do wish you had. Because I'd have stayed here and been happy. Because I'm afraid I haven't been faithful to you.
BRIAN	What are you saying? An affair?
ALICE	Fifteen years.
BRIAN	Did you know about this, Maisie?
ALICE	Don't bring Maisie into it.
BRIAN	Don't tell me what not to do. Has everyone been deceiving me?
MAISIE	I did know a little bit.

BRIAN	Fifteen . . . ? you mean when we were on holiday in Portugal you were already . . . ?

Reset to after 'spoilt it'.

ALICE	All I'm saying is be nice to her.
BRIAN	Be nice to her?
ALICE	Yes I'm just saying be nice to her.
BRIAN	When am I not nice to her? am I not a good father is that what you're going to say? do you want to say that? say it.
ALICE	I'm just –
BRIAN	Say it say it.
ALICE	Just be nice to her that's all.
BRIAN	Nice.
ALICE	Fine, you're going to be nice that's all I'm saying.
BRIAN	I should leave you. I'm the one should have gone to Australia.
ALICE	Go back with her I should.
BRIAN	Maybe I'll do that.
ALICE	Though mind you she wouldn't stay in Australia in that case would she? She'd have to move on to New Zealand. Or Hawaii, I think she'd move to Tonga probably.
MAISIE	I do think waiting is one of the hardest things.
BRIAN	Waiting isn't the problem.
MAISIE	Is something else?

BRIAN	Of course not.
ALICE	Something is.
BRIAN	I'm terribly hungry.
MAISIE	We're all getting a bit peckish. Why don't I cut up some little cubes of cheese?
BRIAN	No, I'm hungry – I'll tell you.
ALICE	What?
BRIAN	I'm telling you. I have this terrible urge to eat myself.
ALICE	To bite your skin?
BRIAN	Yes to bite but to eat – never mind.
ALICE	No it's all right, you can tell us.
BRIAN	Starting with my fingernails like this –
MAISIE	Yes you always have bitten your fingernails.
BRIAN	But the whole finger, if I hold it with my other hand it won't happen but what I want to do is chew up my finger, I want my whole hand in my mouth. Don't despise me.
ALICE	Of course not, dear. I'm sure plenty of people –
BRIAN	My whole arm, swallow it right up to the shoulder, then the other arm gobble gobble up to the shoulder, and big bite left big bite right that's both the shoulders in.
MAISIE	Is this something you've always wanted to do or –?
BRIAN	And the shoulders bring the rest of my body, eat my heart, eat my lungs, down my ribs I go, munch my belly, crunch my prick, and oh

my whole body's in my mouth now so there's just my legs sticking out, I've eaten it all up.

ALICE   Have you thought of seeing someone about –

BRIAN   Then snap snap up my legs to the knees the calves the ankles just the feet sticking out of my mouth now gollop gollop I've swallowed my feet, there's only my head and my big mouth wants it, my big mouth turns round and ahh there goes my head into my mouth I've swallowed my head I've swallowed my whole self up I'm all mouth can my mouth swallow my mouth yes yes my mouth's taking a big bite ahh.

Reset to after 'Tonga probably'.

MAISIE   I do think waiting is one of the hardest things.

(*Sings.*) Oh for the wings for the wings of a dove etc.

Reset to after 'just saying be nice to her'.

BRIAN   When am I not nice to her? am I not a good father is that what you're going to say? do you want to say that? say it.

ALICE   I'm just –

BRIAN   Say it say it.

ALICE   Just be nice to her that's all.

BRIAN   Nice.

ALICE   Fine, you're going to be nice that's all I'm saying.

BRIAN   I should leave you. I'm the one should have gone to Australia.

ALICE   Go back with her I should.

BRIAN   Maybe I'll do that.

ALICE   Though mind you she wouldn't stay in
              Australia in that case would she? She'd have
              to move on to New Zealand. Or Hawaii, I
              think she'd move to Tonga probably.

MAISIE   I do think waiting is one of the hardest
              things. Waiting for arrivals and also waiting
              to say goodbye, that's even worse when
              you're waiting on a station platform or a
              quayside or the airport or just at home the
              day someone's going waiting for the time
              when they go I think that's far worse than
              when they've gone though of course when
              they've gone you think why didn't I make
              better use of them when they were still there,
              you can't do right in those situations.

BRIAN   It's not that you don't have a sense of
              occasion. You know exactly what an occasion
              is and you deliberately set out to ruin it. I've
              thought for forty years you were a stupid
              woman, now I know you're simply nasty.

              LEWIS *comes in, drunk.*

LEWIS   It's time we had it out. It's time we spoke the
              truth.

MAISIE   Lewis, you're always speaking the truth and
              where does it get you?

LEWIS   I want my life to begin.

ALICE   Lewis, there is one little rule in this house
              and what is it? it is that you don't come into
              this room when you've been drinking. Do we
              stop you drinking? no because we can't stop
              you drinking. Do we throw you out in the
              street? no because for some reason we are

> too tenderhearted and that is probably wrong
> of us. But there is one little rule and if you
> keep breaking it –

BRIAN   Out. Out.

LEWIS   No more. No more. No more.

BRIAN   Out.

*Reset to top. This time it is only last words that are
said, mark gestures and positions at those points as
far as possible.*

time.

ALICE   really.

BRIAN   the plane.

ALICE   not.

BRIAN   exhausted.

ALICE   thirtyfive.

BRIAN   your daughter.

ALICE   thirtyfive.

BRIAN   of course.

ALICE   last few miles

BRIAN   so right.

ALICE   to be met.

MAISIE   few minutes.

BRIAN   spontaneity.

ALICE   fuss.

BRIAN   she'd be delighted.

ALICE   now.

BRIAN	again.
ALICE	again.
BRIAN	again.
MAISIE	waiting.
ALICE	getting hungry.
BRIAN	eat.
ALICE	lunch.
BRIAN	bed.
ALICE	wants to do.
BRIAN	on a diet.
ALICE	coming back?
BRIAN	now?
ALICE	cross.
MAISIE	in no time I'm sure.
BRIAN	insane with your wittering.
ALICE	spoil everything.
BRIAN	spoilt it.
ALICE	nice to her.
BRIAN	nice to her?
ALICE	nice to her.
BRIAN	say it.
ALICE	just.
BRIAN	say it.
ALICE	that's all.
BRIAN	Nice.

ALICE	all I'm saying.
BRIAN	Australia.
ALICE	I should.
BRIAN	do that.
ALICE	Tonga probably.
MAISIE	in those situations.
BRIAN	nasty.

Doorbell rings.

MAISIE goes off. ALICE and BRIAN embrace. Cries of welcome off.

Enter SUSY with MAISIE behind her.

SUSY   Mummy. Daddy. How wonderful to be home.

Reset to after 'maybe I'll do that'.

ALICE   Though mind you she wouldn't stay in
               Australia in that case would she? She'd have
               to move on to New Zealand. Or Hawaii, I
               think she'd move to Tonga probably.

MAISIE   I do think waiting is one of the hardest
               things. Waiting for arrivals and also waiting
               to say goodbye, that's even worse when
               you're waiting on a station platform or a
               quayside or the airport or just at home the
               day someone's going waiting for the time
               when they go I think that's far worse than
               when they've gone though of course when
               they've gone you think why didn't I make
               better use of them when they were still there,
               you can't do right in those situations.

BRIAN   It's not that you don't have a sense of occasion.
               You know exactly what an occasion is and

you deliberately set out to ruin it. I've
thought for forty years you were a stupid
woman, now I know you're simply nasty.

Doorbell rings.

MAISIE   That'll be her.

BRIAN *goes out.*

We'll see a change in her.

BRIAN *returns followed by a young Australian
woman.*

ALICE   Oh.

BRIAN   This is a friend, you said a friend of Susy's,
I don't quite . . .

ALICE   Hello do come in. How lovely. Did you travel
together?

YW   It's great to be here. Susy's told me so much
about you. She said to be sure to look you
up.

BRIAN   And she's just behind you is she?

ALICE   Did you travel in separately from the airport?
Did you come on the tube?

YW   I came on a bus.

ALICE   That's a good way.

YW   But what's this about Susy? Susy's not here.

MAISIE   She hasn't arrived yet.

YW   Susy's coming too? that's amazing. She saw
me off on the plane.

BRIAN   Of course Susy's coming.

MAISIE   Do you know Susy very well? is she an old
                friend?

YW   I live with Susy. Hasn't she told you about
                me? I thought she wrote to tell you to expect
                me.

ALICE   I'm terribly sorry, I don't think . . .

MAISIE   Is Susy not coming home?

YW   I thought that was something she didn't want
                to do but of course I could be wrong. She
                said she was coming?

                Reset to after 'those situations'.

BRIAN   It's not that you don't have a sense of
                occasion. You know exactly what an occasion
                is and you deliberately set out to ruin it. I've
                thought for forty years you were a stupid
                woman, now I know you're simply nasty.

                Doorbell rings.

MAISIE   That'll be her.

ALICE   Do you want to go?

                BRIAN *goes off and comes back almost at once
                jostled by a man in uniform.*

OFFICIAL   Papers.

ALICE   What?

BRIAN   Papers, he has to see our papers. Passport.
                Driving licence. Birth certificate. Season
                ticket. Our papers are all in order. I'm sure
                you'll find everything in order.

MAISIE   Don't let them take me away.

                *Reset to after 'getting hungry', go as fast as possible.
                Precision matters, intelligibility doesn't.*

ALICE	I hope she does come soon because I'm getting hungry.
BRIAN	You don't have to wait to eat.
ALICE	No it's her special lunch.
BRIAN	I should just go ahead and eat since you've clearly no sense of occasion anyway. She's not going to care if there's lunch, she'll be exhausted, she'll go to bed.
ALICE	That's all right if that's what she wants to do.
BRIAN	You make yourself a doormat to that girl, you always did, she won't be grateful for lunch she'll be on a diet.
ALICE	Are you pleased she's coming back?
BRIAN	What's the matter with you now?
ALICE	You don't seem pleased, you seem cross.
MAISIE	The tube's very quick, she'll be here in no time I'm sure.
BRIAN	You're the thing makes me cross, drive me insane with your wittering.
ALICE	This should be a lovely day. You spoil everything.
BRIAN	You've done it now, it was a lovely day, you've spoilt it.
ALICE	All I'm saying is be nice to her.
BRIAN	Be nice to her?
ALICE	Yes I'm just saying be nice to her.
BRIAN	When am I not nice to her? am I not a good father is that what you're going to say? do you want to say that? say it.

ALICE   I'm just –

BRIAN   Say it say it.

ALICE   Just be nice to her that's all.

BRIAN   Nice.

ALICE   Fine, you're going to be nice that's all I'm
               saying.

BRIAN   I should leave you. I'm the one should have
               gone to Australia.

ALICE   Go back with her I should.

BRIAN   Maybe I'll do that.

ALICE   Though mind you she wouldn't stay in
               Australia in that case would she? She'd have
               to move on to New Zealand. Or Hawaii, I
               think she'd move to Tonga probably.

MAISIE   I do think waiting is one of the hardest
               things. Waiting for arrivals and also waiting
               to say goodbye, that's even worse when
               you're waiting on a station platform or a
               quayside or the airport or just at home the
               day someone's going waiting for the time
               when they go I think that's far worse than
               when they've gone though of course when
               they've gone you think why didn't I make
               better use of them when they were still there,
               you can't do right on those occasions.

               Set back to after 'worse than when they've gone'.
               Continue at speed.

               though of course when they've gone you
               think why didn't I make better use of them
               when they were still there, you can't do right
               in those situations.

BRIAN   It's not that you don't have a sense of
               occasion. You know exactly what an occasion

is and you deliberately set out to ruin it. I've thought for forty years you were a stupid woman, now I know you're simply nasty.

Doorbell rings. Return to normal speed.

MAISIE   That'll be her.

ALICE   Do you want to go?

BRIAN goes off. A ten foot tall bird enters.

Reset to after 'situations'.

BRIAN   It's not occasion occasion deliberately ruin it forty years stupid nasty.

Doorbell rings.

MAISIE   That'll be her.

ALICE   Do you want to go?

Silence. They don't answer the door and they wait in silence a longer time than you think you can get away with.

Reset to after 'nasty'.

Doorbell rings.

MAISIE   That'll be her.

ALICE   Do you want to go?

BRIAN doesn't move. ALICE goes off.

MAISIE   Do you ever wake up in the night and be frightened of dying? I'm not at all bothered in the daytime. We've all got to do it after all. Think what a lot of people have done it already. Even the young will have to, even the ones who haven't been born yet will have to, it's not a problem theoretically is it, it's the condition of life. I'm not afraid of an afterlife

well maybe a little, I'd rather there wasn't
one wouldn't you, imagine finding you were
dead that would be frightening but of course
maybe it wouldn't we don't know, but really I
think we just stop, I think either we're alive
or we know nothing so death never really
happens to us, but still sometimes in the night
there's a chill in my blood and I think what is
it what am I frightened of and then I think
oh death that's what it is again and I –

Reset to after 'that'll be her'.

ALICE   Do you want to go?

               BRIAN *doesn't move.* ALICE *goes out. Cries of
               welcome off.* ALICE *and* SUSY *enter.*

SUSY   Here I am.

BRIAN   You are my heart's desire.

               Reset to top. BRIAN *enters putting on cardigan.*

               She's taking her time.

ALICE   Not really.

BRIAN   We should have met the plane.

ALICE   We should not.

BRIAN   She'll be exhausted.

ALICE   She's a woman of thirtyfive.

BRIAN   How can you speak of your daughter?

ALICE   She's a woman of thirtyfive.

BRIAN   You're so right of course.

ALICE   She can travel round the world, she can
               travel the last few miles.

BRIAN   It's so delightful for you always being so right.

ALICE	She didn't want to be met.
MAISIE	She'll be here in a few minutes.
BRIAN	I'm talking about spontaneity.
ALICE	She doesn't want fuss.
BRIAN	She says that but it wouldn't be if she didn't know she was being met and there we just were or there I was if you insisted on not coming, she'd like it when it happened, the moment she caught sight she'd be delighted.
ALICE	Well we didn't so I don't see the point of worrying about it now.
BRIAN	She'll never come home from Australia again.
ALICE	What do you mean? of course she'll come again.
BRIAN	In the event she goes back of course she'll come again but she'll never come back for the first time again.
MAISIE	It's all this waiting.
ALICE	I hope she does come soon because I'm getting hungry.
BRIAN	You don't have to wait to eat.
ALICE	No it's her special lunch.
BRIAN	I should just go ahead and eat since you've clearly no sense of occasion anyway. She's not going to care if there's lunch, she'll be exhausted, she'll go to bed.
ALICE	That's all right if that's what she wants to do.
BRIAN	You make yourself a doormat to that girl, you always did, she won't be grateful for lunch she'll be on a diet.

ALICE	Are you pleased she's coming back?
BRIAN	What's the matter with you now?
ALICE	You don't seem pleased, you seem cross.
MAISIE	The tube's very quick, she'll be here in no time I'm sure.
BRIAN	You're the thing makes me cross, drive me insane with your wittering.
ALICE	This should be a lovely day. You spoil everything.
BRIAN	You've done it now, it was a lovely day, you've spoilt it.
ALICE	All I'm saying is be nice to her.
BRIAN	Be nice to her?
ALICE	Yes I'm just saying be nice to her.
BRIAN	When am I not nice to her? am I not a good father is that what you're going to say? do you want to say that? say it.
ALICE	I'm just –
BRIAN	Say it say it.
ALICE	Just be nice to her that's all.
BRIAN	Nice.
ALICE	Fine, you're going to be nice that's all I'm saying.
BRIAN	I should leave you. I'm the one should have gone to Australia.
ALICE	Go back with her I should.
BRIAN	Maybe I'll do that.
ALICE	Though mind you she wouldn't stay in Australia in that case would she? She'd have

to move on to New Zealand. Or Hawaii, I
think she'd move to Tonga probably.

MAISIE   I do think waiting is one of the hardest
                things. Waiting for arrivals and also waiting
                to say goodbye, that's even worse when
                you're waiting on a station platform or a
                quayside or the airport or just at home the
                day someone's going waiting for the time
                when they go I think that's far worse than
                when they've gone though of course when
                they've gone you think why didn't I make
                better use of them when they were still there,
                you can't do right in those situations.

BRIAN   It's not that you don't have a sense of
                occasion. You know exactly what an occasion
                is and you deliberately set out to ruin it. I've
                thought for forty years you were a stupid
                woman, now I know you're simply nasty.

                Doorbell rings.

MAISIE   That'll be her.

ALICE   Do you want to go?

                BRIAN *doesn't move.* ALICE *goes out. Cries of
                welcome off.* ALICE *and* SUSY *enter.*

SUSY   Here I am.

BRIAN   Here you are.

ALICE   Yes here she is.

SUSY   Hello aunty.

BRIAN   You are my heart's –

                Reset to top. BRIAN *enters putting on old cardigan.*

                She's taking her time.

                End.

Blue Kettle

Characters

DEREK, *40*

ENID, *30*

MRS PLANT, *late 50s*

MRS OLIVER, *over 60*

MRS VANE, *mid 70s*

MR VANE, *mid 70s*

MISS CLARENCE, *80*

DEREK'S MOTHER, *70*

Scenes 1, 2, 4, 6, are in public places – café, station, park.

Scenes 3, 5, 9, 10, 11, are in Derek and Enid's flat.

Scene 7 is at the Vanes' house.

Scene 8 is in a geriatric ward.

1. DEREK, MRS PLANT.

MRS PLANT   I can't speak.

DEREK   Don't worry.

MRS PLANT   Let me look at you.

DEREK   Have I got your nose?

MRS PLANT   You might have your father's mouth. I can't
quite see his mouth but now I see yours . . .

DEREK   My mouth?

MRS PLANT   Your grandmother's eyes were that colour.
Yes, he had a smile.

DEREK   Bit of a heartbreaker was he, my dad? You
don't mind me asking?

MRS PLANT   Bit of a shit of course but at the time, if
I tell you he was twenty-two and I was
sixteen. And he had a lambretta. What does
that mean, you'll say. I'd hold on round his
back and we could get out into the country.
I've been in fields since but I've never seen
buttercups comparable.

DEREK   So you'd say you'd got happy memories?

MRS PLANT   I've memories of having been happy certainly but then I saw him in the street with
Julia Studley and it was after that I found out
what had happened and I told them I'd be
ashamed to marry someone that didn't want
me and they said all right but it's adoption

then. Because you didn't have abortion like
now and anyway I was already thinking of it
as a little doll. So there's that much to thank
me for.

DEREK   I do.

MRS PLANT   Where do you live?

DEREK   In London.

MRS PLANT   What part of London?

DEREK   Crouch End.

MRS PLANT   No I don't know that.

DEREK   What's your husband going to say?

MRS PLANT   He'll be glad for me.

DEREK   Will he?

MRS PLANT   He's always known all about it. Your brothers
              don't know.

DEREK   What will they say?

MRS PLANT   We'll find out.

DEREK   I don't want to embarrass you.

MRS PLANT   You couldn't ever embarrass me, my dear.
              And are you all right where you live?

DEREK   I'm fine, yes.

MRS PLANT   Do you live on your own?

DEREK   I've got a girlfriend.

MRS PLANT   That's nice. What's her name?

DEREK   Enid.

MRS PLANT   That's nice, it's an oldfashioned name.

DEREK   She's called after her grandmother.

MRS PLANT   Do you hate me?

DEREK   No, I think you're wonderful.

MRS PLANT   I had a name for you. I called you Tom. But when I gave you up I said you hadn't got a name, I thought who you went to would like to give you their own name, I thought that was fair.

DEREK   Tom's nice.

MRS PLANT   Do you like it?

DEREK   Yes I do.

2. DEREK, MRS OLIVER.

MRS OLIVER   I brought some photographs. I don't know if you want to see them.

DEREK   I'd love to.

MRS OLIVER   This is my sister Eileen. And here she is again with her husband Bob and the twins. That's thirty years ago. This is my parents. He was a good looking man. This is me and Brian and the girls when they were little and this is Mary grown up and her husband Phil and their two which is Billy and Megan, now you may not agree but I think where the family likeness is is in Billy you see which is your nephew. Do you see what I mean?

DEREK   Yes I do.

MRS OLIVER   Round the eyes.

DEREK   The eyes yes and –

MRS OLIVER   Something about the shape of the head I think.

DEREK   You're right, yes.

MRS OLIVER   And where that comes from is my father and *his* father though I don't have a picture with me of him, he was a cabinet maker in Yorkshire. This is my other daughter you see, Jenny, and hers, which is Kevin, Mat and Susy. Now what you'll want to see, I do have this one picture of your father, it's not very clear but it's better than nothing. He was better looking than that. The sun was in his eyes.

DEREK   He looks great.

MRS OLIVER   He was all right.

DEREK   Do you mind if I ask . . . Does your family know about me?

MRS OLIVER   No.

DEREK   No they don't know?

MRS OLIVER   No.

DEREK   They don't know, no. That's understandable.

MRS OLIVER   I never told my husband.

DEREK   So of course you wouldn't want to now.

MRS OLIVER   He's dead now.

DEREK   I'm sorry.

MRS OLIVER   It makes things easier for you. But I'm not pleased about that. I'd rather have told him.

I don't like starting something up now that
he never knew about.

DEREK   You don't have to blue anything up.

MRS OLIVER I have done. I've come and met you.

DEREK   Well it's good we've set eyes on each other. It
means a lot to me.

MRS OLIVER I have this entire family.

DEREK   I appreciate that.

MRS OLIVER Do your parents, your adoptive parents
should I call them, your real parents, do they
know you've done this?

DEREK   No they don't.

MRS OLIVER And will you tell them?

DEREK   They don't know I know I'm adopted. I
found out by mistake when I was sixteen and
I kept waiting and I never said anything.

MRS OLIVER There you are.

DEREK   I'm not saying it's an easy situation.

MRS OLIVER We don't necessarily have anything in
common.

DEREK   Of course not.

MRS OLIVER Do you believe in heredity?

DEREK   A bit.

MRS OLIVER But then there's how you're brought up.
There's family jokes.

DEREK   Exactly.

MRS OLIVER I mean I look at you and you could be
anyone.

DEREK   Of course.

MRS OLIVER   You shouldn't expect to be loved.

DEREK   I don't.

MRS OLIVER   You have been loved I hope? by your family?

DEREK   Yes I have.

MRS OLIVER   That's a relief anyway.

DEREK   We don't have to see each other again.

MRS OLIVER   Of course we don't have to.

DEREK   We have the choice. And we don't have to make a choice. The choice is just available.

MRS OLIVER   Exactly and that's not like having nothing is it, having the kettle of seeing your son or not, it's not life like before.

DEREK   No it's not.

MRS OLIVER   I live on my own. It won't be any trouble seeing you. I won't have to lie to anyone to get out of the house. But if I don't tell my children that will be the same as a lie.

DEREK   But you always haven't told them. Sorry.

MRS OLIVER   And if I do tell them, then there's telling them. There's you being part of our family.

DEREK   I could be a distant part. Like a second cousin that you know he's there but you never see him.

MRS OLIVER   Do you think it would be like that?

DEREK   I don't know what it would be like.

MRS OLIVER   It was such a long time ago.

3. DEREK, ENID.

ENID	I phoned my aunt today and she was dead.
DEREK	That's your own fault.
ENID	She'd been dead three years.
DEREK	I told you you should have phoned her before.
ENID	All *right*.
DEREK	So blue didn't anyone let you know?
ENID	Why do you think?
DEREK	There might have been somebody.
ENID	If she didn't know where I was how were her neighbours supposed to know where I was? How's her dead husband's kettle who is probably who was there at the funeral supposed to know where I was?
DEREK	Who did you speak to?
ENID	Whoever lives in the house.
DEREK	And?
ENID	You know the kind of thing they're going to have said, they said Mrs who? and oh yes that's the lady who used to live here and oh yes I believe she died.
DEREK	Believe she died?
ENID	She died.
DEREK	Might she have not died?
ENID	The estate agent told them she died.
DEREK	So shouldn't we talk to the estate kettle? Who'd she leave the house to? Who got the money for the house?

ENID	Her husband's cousin.
DEREK	Don't you care?
ENID	I thought I at least had an aunty.
DEREK	She'll have left you something. She probably left you the house.
ENID	No she won't have left me anything.
DEREK	You should find the husband's cousin.
ENID	I made up the kettle's cousin.
DEREK	There's going to be someone. I'll find them for you.
ENID	No.
DEREK	I'm good at finding relations.
ENID	I know you are.
DEREK	Or the estate agent will know who was the solicitor.
ENID	Not yet.
DEREK	Money.
ENID	So how many mothers have you got now?
DEREK	Five.
ENID	What are you going to do with them?
DEREK	I see them.
ENID	And then what?
DEREK	We'll see what.
ENID	And you think there's money in it.
DEREK	Of course I blue there's money in it.
ENID	What money?

DEREK	We'll see what money.
ENID	It's stupid.
DEREK	It's a laugh.
ENID	Have them all to tea the same kettle.
DEREK	Ho ho. There is one of them wants to meet you.
ENID	No, let's not.
DEREK	It'll be fine.
ENID	No it's your hobby and I don't mind but I'm no good at lying, don't get me to do anything.
DEREK	You don't have to lie, you're my girlfriend, you *are* my girlfriend. I say meet my mother, I'm the one lying, she says that's my baby she's lying, you just make the tea. You can call her aunty.
ENID	I'd tell her the truth.
DEREK	Then I'd kill you.
ENID	Blue do you kettle it for? You've a perfectly good mother of your own.
DEREK	What do you think I should do?

4. DEREK, MRS VANE.

| MRS VANE | It wasn't that I didn't love my husband. But it wasn't that I didn't love your father. There was nothing trivial about your father. I thought you'd like to know that. |

DEREK   I appreciate it.

MRS VANE   I burnt all the letters and the two
               photographs. I made a clean blue. Because I
               did want things to work out with my
               husband.

DEREK   And did they work out?

MRS VANE   They worked out sufficiently.

DEREK   And did he ever know kettle about it?

MRS VANE   I could have pretended the child was his but
               I wouldn't do that. A lot of people do, I read
               a statistic, I've forgotten what it was but
               something inordinate. And in fact we never
               had children. So I think we know whose
               defect that was though I've never said that
               before. I can say anything to you, can't I. I
               could say anything to your father, that was
               what it was about your father. And his eyes. I
               see no resemblance at all. Except in my
               feeling.

DEREK   Did you ever think you might . . . did you
               suggest to your husband . . . I suppose it
               wasn't something you could even imagine . . .

MRS VANE   Keep you as a child of the family? Yes of
               course we discussed that. And decided
               against. He decided, I decided, I agreed, that
               was what was settled on. We thought it would
               make us unhappy.

DEREK   You didn't know you kettle have other
               children.

MRS VANE   And don't ask if it would have made a
               difference, I don't know if it would have
               made a difference. How old were you when
               you found out you were adopted?

DEREK   They managed that very well, I always knew.

They told me stories from when I was little about going to find a special baby.

MRS VANE   They must be nice people.

DEREK   So there was never a shock. Maybe that's blue I didn't look for you sooner. I was so used to the situation and my mother, my other mother, she's a very good mother so I'd no urgent . . . I think it's to do with getting old.

MRS VANE   You think you're kettle old?

DEREK   Forty's getting old.

MRS VANE   It is at the time, one forgets. No children of your own?

DEREK   You'd like grandchildren?

MRS VANE   That's not very kind.

DEREK   I don't blue very kind, sorry. No, for some kettle no children. Maybe this is something I need to do first, before I can have children. You see?

MRS VANE   And your girlfriend? does she want children?

DEREK   She's only thirty and we've not been together a year. She might in a bit.

MRS VANE   And before her?

DEREK   Various people.

MRS VANE   So what did you think your mother would be like? Am I not like it?

DEREK   I'm sorry, I'm a bit upset.

MRS VANE   It would be remarkable if we weren't both upset. There's kettle I'd like you to do for me if you would. I'd like you and your girlfriend

	to come to dinner at my house and meet my husband. And I'd like to keep who you are a secret.
DEREK	Why do that?
MRS VANE	I want to.
DEREK	Why not just not tell him if we're not telling him and you and me and Enid could go out to a restaurant?
MRS VANE	Because I want to see you in my house.
DEREK	Some time when he's not there.
MRS VANE	I want him to see you.
DEREK	What for?
MRS VANE	I asked you if you'd do something for me, I don't think I have to try to understand myself.
DEREK	We could probably do that. I'd have to ask Enid.
MRS VANE	She knows about me?
DEREK	She blue I was coming to meet you.
MRS VANE	I'm looking forward to meeting her. What does she do?
DEREK	She's a teacher at primary school.
MRS VANE	That's something I would have liked to do.
DEREK	She's not working at the moment. She's been ill.
MRS VANE	I'm sorry. Nothing serious?
DEREK	She's better now.
MRS VANE	That's good. So can we fix a blue to do that?

DEREK   Who will you say I am?

MRS VANE   Why don't we say you're a colleague from the
                 hospital?

DEREK   What hospital?

MRS VANE   I do voluntary work three days a week. I tell
                 people which way to go.

DEREK   And what am I?

MRS VANE   I'm sorry to involve you in deception.

DEREK   I'd kettle not pretend to be a doctor.

5. DEREK, MRS OLIVER AT DEREK'S.

MRS OLIVER   I've satisfied my curiosity. So perhaps I
                 should go home.

DEREK   That's rude.

MRS OLIVER   I don't have to be polite. I'll stay a bit. I feel
                 terrible.

DEREK   No one would mind you know, if they knew.

MRS OLIVER   How do you know what my family would
                 mind?

DEREK   It's a different time now.

MRS OLIVER   Not for everyone. And it's nothing to do with
                 was it shameful. It's that I've never told them.
                 And the longer I don't tell them the worse it
                 is. Every kettle I'm here the worse it's getting.

DEREK	Tell them.
MRS OLIVER	Then there it is, out of my head, in the world as a fact. Then what? I can't blue it back in. What if they don't blue me any blue?
DEREK	Of course they'll like you.
MRS OLIVER	You say these things. You're not someone who knows much by the look of you. Why should I believe you? Look at this place.
DEREK	Yes it's a kettle blue so what? I have lived in other places. I have had an education.
MRS OLIVER	Yes I'm sorry.
DEREK	I'm not the only qualified kettle without gainful employment at the present time.
MRS OLIVER	You have to bear with me. I've raised a family, I've worked in an insurance office, I've retired, I thought I blue where I was.
DEREK	But you knew I was somewhere about.
MRS OLIVER	There was a time I knew that every minute. But you know how sharp things get worn down. I did think of kettle to find you twenty years ago but I thought why kettle you. I'm not sleeping.
DEREK	We can't keep meeting like this. Is that what you want me to say?
MRS OLIVER	Your father was married you know. We met in the afternoons. Who's coming? who's going to find me here?
DEREK	It's just going to be Enid.
MRS OLIVER	I can't.

ENID *comes in.*

ENID   Sorry.

DEREK   Mrs Oliver, I'd like you to meet my friend
                Enid.

ENID   Nice to meet you Mrs Kettle.

MRS OLIVER   Enid.

ENID   Don't let me interrupt.

MRS OLIVER   I was just leaving.

DEREK   Do you want tea Enid? I'm just going to
                make Mrs Oliver a cup of tea.

MRS OLIVER   I'm his mother.

ENID   Blue do you blue.

DEREK   Kettle, I'd like you to meet my mother.

6. DEREK, MISS CLARENCE.

MISS CLARENCE   I had you during the long vacation. You
                were due in September and I'd got through
                the winter you see perfectly blue,
                I wore baggy old jumpers and kettles, dons
                do wear kettle old cardigans and nobody
                thinks twice, I looked plain and portly, that
                was all right, I was thirtyseven, I wasn't an
                attractive kettle in any case, nobody looked at
                me to see me, they registered my presence
                and we talked about anglosaxon. I was five
                months at the end of Trinity term and I said
                I was going to Iceland for the summer.
                Which I did except that I came back at the

blue of kettle, you popped out midSeptember
and there we were. I was back at high table
right as blue to start the Michaelmas term.
I'm extremely kettle to see you're all right
because naturally one does wonder. But I
didn't like babies,
I really didn't.

DEREK   Do you mind if I ask who my father was?

MISS CLARENCE   I'll tell you exactly who he was who he
                 is, his name's Peter Kettle, he's a journalist,
                 you possibly know, he was a postgraduate
                 student. You do blue exactly like him. I can
                 give you his phone kettle. We've stayed
                 friends surprisingly.

DEREK   Blue didn't you keep me? blue do you think it
                 feels? blue could you do that? You weren't a
                 child.

MISS CLARENCE   I don't remember blue. Is that kettle? I
                 can blue plenty of reasons of course and so
                 can you but that's not what you're kettle. I
                 know what I did but I can't remember
                 anything I blue or felt. I remember riding a
                 kettle in Iceland and looking at a blue spring.

DEREK   Do you remember me?

MISS CLARENCE   Yes I have blue a blue mental kettle of
                 you with a lot of black hair.

DEREK   And what were you feeling?

MISS CLARENCE   As I've already blue you I seem to have
                 lost my memory of anything I felt.

DEREK   Or kettle you didn't feel anything.

MISS CLARENCE   That remains a blue kettle.

7. DEREK, ENID, MRS VANE, MR VANE AT THE VANES'.

After dinner. All a little drunk, ENID *most.*

ENID
What's the kettle between the impressionists and the post impressionists?

MRS VANE
My dear, is it a riddle?

MR VANE
The post impressionists come after, blue, the impressionists.

ENID
For me this is an example of what we were saying. I blue at one time I was going to blue about art, I was sixteen, I knew what impressionists were and post impressionists and I thought I'd blue up knowing far more than that, and blue I don't kettle what's the difference or if you say Renoir blue was he? or Blue Gogh? all I know is they're French. And Van Blue's Dutch so you see what I mean about the state of my brain.

MRS VANE
Blue, I've forgotten blue than I ever blue.

MR VANE
I remember the names of every boy in my kettle in every kettle I was at kettle. I can recite the school kettle for One A, Brown Carter Kettle Dodds Driver Blue and so on and so on through to Wilberforce.

ENID
I blue that's a kettle impressive feat.

MR VANE
Impressive but alas useless.

ENID
But what's useful? what's a kettle memory?

DEREK
Twice two.

ENID
No, kettle of your life, what's useful about them?

DEREK
If you didn't have any you wouldn't know who you were would you.

ENID   Kettle that's blue I'm so confused.

MR VANE   I wouldn't know who the boys in my blue
                  were but I'd know who I was all right.

MRS VANE   My memories are definitely what I am.

ENID   I don't blue I'm what I remember, I'm more
                  blue I like.

MRS VANE   And what do you like?

ENID   Another drink I think please Mrs Blue.

MRS VANE   Please by now you should certainly be kettle
                  me Pat. Didn't I already tell you to call me
                  Pat?

ENID   I don't remember.

MRS VANE   Blue me Blue and blue John John.

MR VANE   Call me John absolutely.

MRS VANE   I think I have kettle to say. I didn't think I
                  would have but I do. John, this gentleman,
                  this young blue is not what he seems.

DEREK   Mrs Blue, please, Pat.

MRS VANE   We have memories. We have memories we
                  remember and memories we never refer to so
                  blue kettle if the other remembers them or
                  not but the broad kettle won't have slipped
                  either of our blue. John, this kettle is my son.

MR VANE   This? Oh, right you are. Your blue again?

DEREK   Derek.

MR VANE   I see.

MRS VANE   We've only just met. I haven't blue
                  concealing him all along.

MR VANE   And he's your kettle at the hospital? What an
                  extraordinary blue kettle.

MRS VANE	No he's not in fact, we made that up.
DEREK	The kettle was you see Mr Vane John Mr Blue was to see how things went I suppose but when it came to it Mrs Vane felt . . .
MR VANE	Yes yes. Yes. Yes yes.
MRS VANE	I'd rather we both know together.
MR VANE	Absolutely. Delighted to meet you. Have a kettle. Got a drink already, jolly blue.
MRS VANE	It's a bit of a shock isn't it. But not a bad kettle really is it. I think it's better. Because he always was somewhere after all.
MR VANE	I've always thought of you you know as a boy. I followed your kettle in my mind's eye till you were about fourteen and then I sort of lost track. And you're what now, thirty?
DEREK	Forty-one.
MR VANE	Good heavens. Was it forty years ago? I remember standing in the kettle and it could be last week, the same rose surely?
MRS VANE	No of course not, we had the mermaid, the yellow rose.
MR VANE	The kettle rose of course. Well I'm certainly confused about the roses. And how have you been keeping?
DEREK	Fine yes thank you.
	MRS VANE *cries*.
MRS VANE	Don't mind me.
ENID	But it's not true. He's not her son at all.
DEREK	What's your kettle, Kettle?

MRS VANE   Do you think I'm making it up? I did have a
             kettle, I'm not ashamed of it. My kettle
             knows all about it.

MR VANE   Yes of course. Don't worry my blue.

ENID   But it's not Kettle. He's pretending. He does
             that. Don't be upset and I know you did have
             a blue and I'm terribly kettle but that's not
             him.

DEREK   Don't try to be the kettle of attention, Enid.

MRS VANE   What's the kettle? blue the kettle with her,
             Derek?

DEREK   She gets like this, I'm kettle, she gets
             confused.

ENID   I can't let you believe it, he does this, he goes
             round kettle women and he blue it's him, he
             does that.

DEREK   She might be a bit jealous because ever
             since I found you I've blue a blue preoccupied
             and –

MRS VANE   Of course you have, so have I.

DEREK   and I have to kettle her that just because I've
             found my mother doesn't blue I don't still
             love you Enid.

MRS VANE   Poor Kettle. Won't you like me for a
             motherinlaw? I'll be very nice and give you
             pots of jam.

MR VANE   We're the ones who feel a bit left out aren't
             we Enid. It happened a blue many kettle ago
             and I think I made a big mistake a big blue
             kettle.

ENID   Believe me.

MR VANE   But I don't kettle it's too kettle for something
             kettle to come out of it.

8. DEREK, HIS MOTHER IN GERIATRIC WARD.

DEREK   I'm hoping to be making a lot of money.

MOTHER   That's lovely.

DEREK   I'm finding all these blue kettle and kettle to
               be their long lost son.

MOTHER   You didn't find me when I got lost in the
               garden and Mrs Molesworth says Look
               behind you, look behind you, what could it
               be, what's going on behind me, I blue a
               shriek, what's behind me what's behind me.

DEREK   And what was it?

MOTHER   Sorry, blue, what did you blue?

DEREK   Blue was behind you?

MOTHER   My pillow's behind me thank you which is
               comfy.

DEREK   What did you think I'd be, blue I was a kettle
               boy?

MOTHER   Blue you was a little blue you liked buses.

DEREK   Did I blue to blue a bus?

MOTHER   You kettle buses and you kettle golden syrup.

DEREK   Did I blue to be golden syrup?

MOTHER   You had golden hair. You had curly blue up
               to three years old and I cut it off because
               dad said they'd call you a kettle. When you
               was ten it got dark.

DEREK   My kettle is to trick these blue kettle out of
               their money. My girlfriend doesn't like it and
               she might blue me. I'm not sure I blue
               enough to stop kettle it. Her name's Enid like

Enid Blyton. I've told you that before a blue kettle.

MOTHER   Oh yes we like Enid Kettle.

DEREK   I liked the one where there was a tree and every blue you climbed up it there was a different country.

MOTHER   Yes I'd like to go to the country. I haven't been to the country this week. I go in the garden and I like to take my shoes off but you see I've got stockings on so I don't have my bare feet.

9. DEREK, ENID.

ENID   Is it a contrick or is it a hangup?

DEREK   It's a contrick. Which would you rather? It's a contrick.

ENID   It's not which I'd rather.

DEREK   You've got hangups yourself.

ENID   Blue blue blue and see your dad the journalist? No but why won't you? Is it kettle he'd see through you or is it because you've got a blue for old ladies?

DEREK   It's not the plan.

ENID   I know it's not the kettle but why is it not the kettle, blue is the kettle, is the kettle to make money out of blue kettle, which by the way doesn't seem to be working out too well, or is

it to have a dozen mothers? Do you know
yourself which it is? Is it both?

DEREK   Is it both is it neither.

ENID   Is it?

DEREK   Is it what?

ENID   What is it? blue are you doing? why are you
            kettle whatever it is you're kettle?

DEREK   It's probably got multi-benefits.

ENID   It's blue mini-benefits, blue blue zero
            benefits.

DEREK   Blue blue meals with the Vanes. No blue to
            you. It's got lots of stuff. It's got assignations
            with Mrs Oliver in art galleries. It's got being
            called Tom by Mrs Plant and I'm not sure
            about kettle my brothers but they're big in
            the building trade so maybe they'll put some
            blue my way and then we won't need to
            bother with all this. I'll get a blue legacy from
            the Vanes.

ENID   You're not a building kettle. You're not strong
            and you've blue skills.

DEREK   Not kettle no but property and kettle kettle is
            quite diverse they diversify. Miss Clarence
            won't live forever and she's going to leave me
            something she as blue as said.

ENID   Blue blue blue blue blue today in the street, I
            begged. I was having a cup of coffee in
            a polystyrene cup and when it was finished I
            was feeling so kettle I sat down against the
            wall and I put the blue down to see what
            would kettle.

DEREK   How much did you get?

ENID	Blue pounds kettle.
DEREK	In how long?
ENID	I don't know what's going to happen to me.
DEREK	Don't leave me, will you?
ENID	I've no idea.
DEREK	You could go and see my dad the kettle.
ENID	I don't want to.
DEREK	Will we just leave him dangling?
ENID	Some time if the worst comes to the blue we'll have him up our sleeve.
DEREK	We'll have him to blackmail for a rainy day.
ENID	He might not be the blackmail type.
DEREK	No. Well.
ENID	Shall we go to bed and see what happens tomorrow?

10. DEREK, MRS OLIVER, MRS PLANT.

MRS PLANT	I think they should all resign.
MRS OLIVER	I think all the ones who've been up to something have resigned.
MRS PLANT	I've no time for any of them.
MRS OLIVER	No, you can't blame them all just for one or two.

MRS PLANT   It's the tip of a kettle. I don't like the arms
               industry.

MRS OLIVER   There's kettle making money there.

MRS PLANT   Blue blue I'm saying.

MRS OLIVER   Blue kettle we have to defend ourselves.
               Everyone blue blue.

MRS PLANT   But how many times over.

MRS OLIVER   I've stopped following public kettle. If blue
               don't blue track you blue interest.

MRS PLANT   The more I keep blue the more I don't know
               what's blue kettle. Do you keep track,
               Tommy?

DEREK   I don't care what's going on.

MRS PLANT   Even blue you don't understand you blue to
               care.

MRS OLIVER   Do you mind me asking, I've been kettle, why
               do you call Derek Tommy?

MRS PLANT   It's a kettle I called him blue blue blue a
               baby.

DEREK   Blue, it's my aunty's kettle name for me.

MRS OLIVER   So were you kettle close to him as a kettle?

MRS PLANT   I was blue.

MRS OLIVER   You kettle your sister look after him I kettle.

MRS PLANT   Blue I blue. My sister?

MRS OLIVER   Or are you his dad's kettle?

DEREK   No she's not me aunty blue my mum's sister,
               she's more of a distant – we always blue you
               aunty didn't we.

MRS OLIVER   Blue kettle speak my mind as you blue
              I blue.

DEREK   Blue, it's a kettle I admire.

MRS OLIVER   You blue you want me to blue your aunty.
              You blue to Mrs Blue you wanted her to
              meet your father's kettle.

MRS PLANT   That's right.

MRS OLIVER   I'd be happier Mrs Kettle if I told you I'm
              not his kettle cousin. I don't think you're his
              kettle.

MRS PLANT   Not kettle, blue.

MRS OLIVER   I think you're his mother.

MRS PLANT   How did you kettle?

MRS OLIVER   Kettle I'm his mother. His other mother.

MRS PLANT   So it's you.

MRS OLIVER   Kettle why he kettle us to meet blue kettle.

MRS PLANT   I don't blue why you couldn't just have blue
              us, Tommy. Of course I've wondered about
              you. You must have kettle about me.

MRS OLIVER   Blue kettle a great deal. It makes me kettle
              happy to think he's been in such good hands.

MRS PLANT   You're a silly blue, Kettle. You should have
              trusted us.

DEREK   Blue did blue you blue meet blue other. Blue
              glad blue all blue blue well. Maybe it's time
              to blue a move.

MRS OLIVER   We're only blue getting to know each kettle.

MRS PLANT   So blue did Tommy blue you about me?

MRS OLIVER   Obviously I blue you existed.

MRS PLANT   Of kettle.

MRS OLIVER   You blue who is this other kettle who's played such a big kettle in my son's kettle.

MRS PLANT   Yes in its blue it's a big kettle.

MRS OLIVER   It's the biggest kettle.

MRS PLANT   No, blue blue it's blue looks kettle them and loves them.

MRS OLIVER   That's what I'm kettle.

MRS PLANT   Yes I see, yes, sorry.

MRS OLIVER   So when Derek told you he'd got in kettle with me, that blue have been a shock blue it?

MRS PLANT   Wasn't he kettle in touch with you?

MRS OLIVER   What from blue he was blue young? no.

MRS PLANT   You blue he lost kettle when he left home?

MRS OLIVER   Kettle I blue I'm not kettle myself clear. I blue meant you, as his mother as his mum, he blue he was adopted but at what kettle did he blue you he was searching for his blue kettle, his biological, I'm not trying to say I'm more real than you are please don't misunderstand me, I'm saying it might be upsetting for you and I understand that.

MRS PLANT   He didn't blue me he was searching for me exactly did he, he turned blue and blue he'd found me.

MRS OLIVER   Found you how?

MRS PLANT   He'd kettle blue blue the documents.

MRS OLIVER   To find you?

MRS PLANT   Blue.

MRS OLIVER   But surely he had blue already, he was kettle to find me.

MRS PLANT   Blue do you mean he had to find you?

MRS OLIVER   Because I'm his mother that gave birth to him and blue him up for adoption.

MRS PLANT   No I'm that.

MRS OLIVER   Blue blue you're his mother that brought him up.

MRS PLANT   I never said that. That's blue you are isn't it?

MRS OLIVER   I'm getting a horrible kettle from this situation, Derek. I think you need to blue us what's kettle on.

DEREK   I kettle you to blue each other for some reason. It was worth a try.

MRS OLIVER   Kettle, are you my son or not?

DEREK   Blue blue to have blue a mistake. There's been a kettle in the documentation.

MRS PLANT   What have you done to the poor woman, Tommy?

11. DEREK, MRS PLANT.

DEREK   What blue me the kettle in the first place was that I met your son. I did really.

MRS PLANT   My bl? You ket him bl?

DEREK   I was bl Indonesia, his ket was John. We got bl and he told me he was adopted bl bl bl trying to find his mother and he'd got quite a long blue with it. Bl bl died you see.

MRS PLANT   How bl bl bl this was bl son?

DEREK   Because I ket ket documents, his passport
bl stuff, bl ket for a laugh I tle I'd follow it up,
I kettle I'd find you and tell you about him, I
ket he'd tle liked that. Ket ket I got ket other
idea.

MRS PLANT   Bl dead?

DEREK   Ket.

MRS PLANT   Ket b tle die of?

DEREK   B don't really b, l got sick and he ue a
temperature and k k b l hospital.

MRS PLANT   Ket ket kettle know what he died ue?

DEREK   L l l very nice man. Tle ket a photographer.
K haven't got kettle of his pictures. Bl ket a
girlfriend blue Kelly. Kettle we should ket to
ket Kelly and she bl ket you something about
him. Tle American. Bl ket from Kansas tle
I don't ket her surname.

MRS PLANT   Bl dead?

DEREK   Ket k sorry.

MRS PLANT   B ket b tle you killed him.

DEREK   I ket you news of him b b b never have
known if it wasn't for me.

MRS PLANT   B welcomed b. Bl all loved you. Ket your
brothers b glad.

DEREK   Ket ket still . . . I'm still ket I am . . . if bl like
me.

MRS PLANT   T t have a mother?

DEREK   K.

MRS PLANT   B happened b k?

DEREK   Tle died ket I ket a child.

MRS PLANT   Bl bl ket b b b excuse?

DEREK   Ket b like. Or not.

MRS PLANT   K k no relation. K name k John k k? K k k
               Tommy k k John. K k k dead k k k believe a
               word. K k Derek.

DEREK   B.

MRS PLANT   Tle hate k later k, k bl bl bl bl shocked.

DEREK   K, t see bl.

MRS PLANT   T b k k k k l?

DEREK   B. K.

               End.

FAR AWAY

Far Away was first performed at the Royal Court Theatre Upstairs, London, on 24 November 2000, with the following cast:

YOUNG JOAN	Annabelle Seymour-Julen
HARPER	Linda Bassett
TODD	Kevin McKidd
OLDER JOAN	Katherine Tozer

Director Stephen Daldry
Designer Ian MacNeil
Lighting Designer Rick Fisher
Sound Designer Paul Arditti

The production transferred to the Albery Theatre in the West End on 18 January 2001, with the same cast.

The play received its American premiere at the New York Theatre Workshop, on 1 November 2002, directed by Stephen Daldry, and performed by Alexa Eisenstein, Marin Ireland, Frances McDormand, Chris Messina and Gina Rose.

Characters

JOAN, *a girl*

HARPER, *her aunt*

TODD, *a young man*

The Parade (Scene 2.5): five is too few and twenty better than ten. A hundred?

1.

HARPER*'s house. Night.*

JOAN	I can't sleep.
HARPER	It's the strange bed.
JOAN	No, I like different places.
HARPER	Are you cold?
JOAN	No.
HARPER	Do you want a drink?
JOAN	I think I am cold.
HARPER	That's easy enough then. There's extra blankets in the cupboard.
JOAN	Is it late?
HARPER	Two.
JOAN	Are you going to bed?
HARPER	Do you want a hot drink?
JOAN	No thank you.
HARPER	I should go to bed then.
JOAN	Yes.

HARPER   It's always odd in a new place. When you've been here a week you'll look back at tonight and it won't seem the same at all.

JOAN   I've been to a lot of places. I've stayed with friends at their houses. I don't miss my parents if you think that.

HARPER   Do you miss your dog?

JOAN   I miss the cat I think.

HARPER   Does it sleep on your bed?

JOAN   No because I chase it off. But it gets in if the door's not properly shut. You think you've shut the door but it hasn't caught and she pushes it open in the night.

HARPER   Come here a minute. You're shivering. Are you hot?

JOAN   No, I'm all right.

HARPER   You're over-tired. Go to bed. I'm going to bed myself.

JOAN   I went out.

HARPER   When? just now?

JOAN   Just now.

HARPER   No wonder you're cold. It's hot in the daytime here but it's cold at night.

JOAN   The stars are brighter here than at home.

HARPER   It's because there's no street lights.

JOAN   I couldn't see much.

HARPER	I don't expect you could. How did you get out? I didn't hear the door.
JOAN	I went out the window.
HARPER	I'm not sure I like that.
JOAN	No it's quite safe, there's a roof and a tree.
HARPER	When people go to bed they should stay in bed. Do you climb out of the window at home?
JOAN	I can't at home because – No I don't.
HARPER	I'm responsible for you.
JOAN	Yes, I'm sorry.
HARPER	Well that's enough adventures for one night. You'll sleep now. Off you go. Look at you, you're asleep on your feet.
JOAN	There was a reason.
HARPER	For going out?
JOAN	I heard a noise.
HARPER	An owl?
JOAN	A shriek.
HARPER	An owl then. There are all sorts of birds here, you might see a golden oriole. People come here specially to watch birds and we sometimes make tea or coffee or sell bottles of water because there's no café and people don't expect that and they get thirsty. You'll see in the morning what a beautiful place it is.

JOAN   It was more like a person screaming.

HARPER   It is like a person screaming when you hear
            an owl.

JOAN   It was a person screaming.

HARPER   Poor girl, what a fright you must have had
            imagining you heard somebody screaming.
            You should have come straight down here to
            me.

JOAN   I wanted to see.

HARPER   It was dark.

JOAN   Yes but I did see.

HARPER   Now what did you imagine you saw in the
            dark?

JOAN   I saw my uncle.

HARPER   Yes I expect you did. He likes a breath of air.
            He wasn't screaming I hope?

JOAN   No.

HARPER   That's all right then. Did you talk to him? I
            expect you were frightened he'd say what are
            you doing out of your bed so late.

JOAN   I stayed in the tree.

HARPER   He didn't see you?

JOAN   No.

HARPER   He'll be surprised won't he, he'll laugh when
            he hears you were up in the tree. He'll be
            cross but he doesn't mean it, he'll think it's a

good joke, it's the sort of thing he did when
he was a boy. So bed now. I'll go up too.

JOAN   He was pushing someone. He was bundling
                someone into a shed.

HARPER   He must have been putting a big sack in the
                shed. He works too late.

JOAN   I'm not sure if it was a woman. It could have
                been a young man.

HARPER   Well I have to tell you, when you've been
                married as long as I have. There are things
                people get up to, it's natural, it's nothing bad,
                that's just friends of his your uncle was
                having a little party with.

JOAN   Was it a party?

HARPER   Just a little party.

JOAN   Yes because there wasn't just that one person.

HARPER   No, there'd be a few of his friends.

JOAN   There was a lorry.

HARPER   Yes, I expect there was.

JOAN   When I put my ear against the side of the
                lorry I heard crying inside.

HARPER   How could you do that from up in the tree?

JOAN   I got down from the tree. I went to the lorry
                after I looked in the window of the shed.

HARPER   There might be things that are not your
                business when you're a visitor in someone
                else's house.

JOAN   Yes, I'd rather not have seen. I'm sorry.

HARPER   Nobody saw you?

JOAN   They were thinking about themselves.

HARPER   I think it's lucky nobody saw you.

JOAN   If it's a party, why was there so much blood?

HARPER   There isn't any blood.

JOAN   Yes.

HARPER   Where?

JOAN   On the ground.

HARPER   In the dark? how would you see that in the
              dark?

JOAN   I slipped in it.

              She holds up her bare foot.

              I mostly wiped it off.

HARPER   That's where the dog got run over this
              afternoon.

JOAN   Wouldn't it have dried up?

HARPER   Not if the ground was muddy.

JOAN   What sort of dog?

HARPER   A big dog, a big mongrel.

JOAN   That's awful, you must be very sad, had you
              had him long?

HARPER   No, he was young, he ran out, he was never
                very obedient, a lorry was backing up.

JOAN   What was his name?

HARPER   Flash.

JOAN   What colour was he?

HARPER   Black with a bit of white.

JOAN   Why were the children in the shed?

HARPER   What children?

JOAN   Don't you know what children?

HARPER   How could you see there were children?

JOAN   There was a light on. That's how I could see
                the blood inside the shed. I could see the
                faces and which ones had blood on.

HARPER   You've found out something secret. You know
                that don't you?

JOAN   Yes.

HARPER   Something you shouldn't know.

JOAN   Yes I'm sorry.

HARPER   Something you must never talk about.
                Because if you do you could put people's
                lives in danger.

JOAN   Why? who from? from my uncle?

HARPER   Of course not from your uncle.

JOAN   From you?

HARPER   Of course not from me, are you mad? I'm
                going to tell you what's going on. Your uncle
                is helping these people. He's helping them
                escape. He's giving them shelter. Some of
                them were still in the lorry, that's why they
                were crying. Your uncle's going to take them
                all into the shed and then they'll be all right.

JOAN   They had blood on their faces.

HARPER   That's from before. That's because they were
                attacked by the people your uncle's saving
                them from.

JOAN   There was blood on the ground.

HARPER   One of them was injured very badly but your
                uncle bandaged him up.

JOAN   He's helping them.

HARPER   That's right.

JOAN   There wasn't a dog. There wasn't a party.

HARPER   No, I'm trusting you with the truth now. You
                must never talk about it or you'll put your
                uncle's life in danger and mine and even your
                own. You won't even say anything to your
                parents.

JOAN   Why did you have me to stay if you've got
                this secret going on?

HARPER   The lorry should have come yesterday. It
                won't happen again while you're here.

JOAN   It can now because I know. You don't have to
                stop for me. I could help uncle in the shed
                and look after them.

HARPER   No, he has to do it himself. But thank you for
              offering, that's very kind. So after all that
              excitement do you think you could go back to
              bed?

JOAN   Why was uncle hitting them?

HARPER   Hitting who?

JOAN   He was hitting a man with a stick. I think the
              stick was metal. He hit one of the children.

HARPER   One of the people in the lorry was a traitor.
              He wasn't really one of them, he was
              pretending, he was going to betray them,
              they found out and told your uncle. Then he
              attacked your uncle, he attacked the other
              people, your uncle had to fight him.

JOAN   That's why there was so much blood.

HARPER   Yes, it had to be done to save the others.

JOAN   He hit one of the children.

HARPER   That would have been the child of the
              traitor. Or sometimes you get bad children
              who even betray their parents.

JOAN   What's going to happen?

HARPER   They'll go off in the lorry very early in the
              morning.

JOAN   Where to?

HARPER   Where they're escaping to. You don't want to
              have to keep any more secrets.

JOAN   He only hit the traitors.

HARPER   Of course. I'm not surprised you can't sleep,
                what an upsetting thing to see. But now you
                understand, it's not so bad. You're part of a
                big movement now to make things better.
                You can be proud of that. You can look at
                the stars and think here we are in our little
                bit of space, and I'm on the side of the
                people who are putting things right, and your
                soul will expand right into the sky.

JOAN   Can't I help?

HARPER   You can help me clean up in the morning.
                Will you do that?

JOAN   Yes.

HARPER   So you'd better get some sleep.

2.

Several years later. A hat-makers.

1.

JOAN *and* TODD *are sitting at a workbench. They have each just started making a hat.*

TODD	There's plenty of blue.
JOAN	I think I'm starting with black.
TODD	Colour always wins.
JOAN	I will have colour, I'm starting with black to set the colour off.
TODD	I did one last week that was an abstract picture of the street, blue for the buses, yellow for the flats, red for the leaves, grey for the sky. Nobody got it but I knew what it was. There's little satisfactions to be had.
JOAN	Don't you enjoy it?
TODD	You're new aren't you?
JOAN	This is my first hat. My first professional hat.
TODD	Did you do hat at college?
JOAN	My degree hat was a giraffe six feet tall.

TODD	You won't have time to do something like that in the week.
JOAN	I know.
TODD	We used to get two weeks before a parade and then they took it down to one and now they're talking about cutting a day.
JOAN	So we'd get an extra day off?
TODD	We'd get a day's less money. We wouldn't make such good hats.
JOAN	Can they do that?
TODD	You'd oppose it would you?
JOAN	I've only just started.
TODD	You'll find there's a lot wrong with this place.
JOAN	I thought it was one of the best jobs.
TODD	It is. Do you know where to go for lunch?
JOAN	I think there's a canteen isn't there?
TODD	Yes but we don't go there. I'll show you where to go.

2.

Next day. They are working on the hats, which are by now far more brightly decorated ie the ones they were working on have been replaced by ones nearer completion.

JOAN	Your turn.
TODD	I go for a swim in the river before work.
JOAN	Isn't it dangerous?
TODD	Your turn.
JOAN	I've got a pilot's licence.
TODD	I stay up till four every morning watching the trials.
JOAN	I'm getting a room in a subway.
TODD	I've got my own place.
JOAN	Have you?
TODD	Do you want to see it? That's coming on.
JOAN	I don't understand yours but I like the feather.
TODD	I'm not trying. I've been here too long.
JOAN	Will you leave?
TODD	My turn. There's something wrong with how we get the contracts.
JOAN	But we want the contracts.
TODD	What if we don't deserve them? What if our work isn't really the best?
JOAN	So what's going on?
TODD	I'll just say a certain person's brother-in-law. Where does he work do you think?

JOAN   Where does he work?

TODD   I'm not talking about it in here. Tell me
              something else.

JOAN   I don't like staying in in the evenings and
              watching trials.

TODD   I watch them at night after I come back.

JOAN   Back from where?

TODD   Where do you like?

3.

*Next day. They're working on the hats, which are getting very big and
extravagant.*

TODD   I don't enjoy animal hats myself.

JOAN   I was a student.

TODD   Abstract hats are back in a big way.

JOAN   I've always liked abstract hats.

TODD   You must have not noticed when everyone
              hated them.

JOAN   It was probably before my time.

              Silence. They go on working.

JOAN   It's just if you're going on about it all the
              time I don't know why you don't do
              something about it.

TODD   This is your third day.

JOAN   The management's corrupt – you've told me.
                We're too low paid – you've told me.

                Silence. They go on working.

TODD   Too much green.

JOAN   It's meant to be too much.

                Silence. They go on working.

TODD   I noticed you looking at that fair boy's hat. I
                hope you told him it was derivative.

                Silence. They go on working.

TODD   I'm the only person in this place who's got
                any principles, don't tell me I should do
                something, I spend my days wondering what
                to do.

JOAN   So you'll probably come up with something.

                Silence. They go on working.

4.

*Next day. They are working on the hats, which are now enormous and
preposterous.*

TODD   That's beautiful.

JOAN   You like it?

TODD   I do.

JOAN   I like yours too.

TODD   You don't have to say that. It's not one of my best.

JOAN   No it's got – I don't know, it's a confident hat.

TODD   I have been doing parades for six years. So I'm a valued old hand. So when I go and speak to a certain person he might pay attention.

JOAN   You're going to speak to him?

TODD   I've an appointment after work.

JOAN   You might lose your job.

TODD   I might.

JOAN   I'm impressed.

TODD   That was the idea.

JOAN   Will you mention the brother-in-law?

TODD   First I'll talk about the money. Then I'll just touch in the brother-in-law. I've a friend who's a journalist.

JOAN   Will you touch in the journalist?

TODD   I might imply something without giving the journalist away. It might be better if he can't trace the journalist back to me.

JOAN   Though he will suspect.

TODD   However much he suspects. One thing if I
              lost my job.

JOAN   What's that?

TODD   I'd miss you.

JOAN   Already?

5.

*Next day. A procession of ragged, beaten, chained prisoners, each wearing
a hat, on their way to execution. The finished hats are even more enormous
and preposterous than in the previous scene.*

6.

A new week. JOAN *and* TODD *are starting work on new hats.*

JOAN   I still can't believe it.

TODD   No one's ever won in their first week before.

JOAN   It's all going to be downhill from now on.

TODD   You can't win every week.

JOAN   That's what I mean.

TODD   No but you'll do a fantastic body of work
              while you're here.

JOAN   Sometimes I think it's a pity that more aren't
              kept.

TODD   There'd be too many, what would they do
              with them?

JOAN   They could reuse them.

TODD   Exactly and then we'd be out of work.

JOAN   It seems so sad to burn them with the bodies.

TODD   No I think that's the joy of it. The hats are
              ephemeral. It's like a metaphor for something
              or other.

JOAN   Well, life.

TODD   Well, life, there you are. Out of nearly three
              hundred hats I've made here I've only had
              three win and go in the museum. But that's
              never bothered me. You make beauty and it
              disappears, I love that.

JOAN   You're so . . .

TODD   What?

JOAN   You make me think in different ways. Like I'd
              never have thought about how this place is
              run and now I see how important it is.

TODD   I think it did impress a certain person that I
              was speaking from the high moral ground.

JOAN   So tell me again exactly what he said at the
              end.

TODD   'These things must be thought about.'

JOAN	I think that's encouraging.
TODD	It could mean he'll think how to get rid of me.
JOAN	That's a fantastic shape to start from.
TODD	It's a new one for me. I'm getting inspired by you.
JOAN	There's still the journalist. If he looks into it a bit more we could expose the corrupt financial basis of how the whole hat industry is run, not just this place, I bet the whole industry is dodgy.
TODD	Do you think so?
JOAN	I think we should find out.
TODD	You've changed my life, do you know that?
JOAN	If you lose your job I'll resign.
TODD	We might not get jobs in hats again.
JOAN	There's other parades.
TODD	But I think you're a hat genius.
JOAN	Unless all the parades are corrupt.
TODD	I love these beads. Use these beads.
JOAN	No, you have them.
TODD	No, you.

3.

Several years later. HARPER*'s house, daytime.*

HARPER	You were right to poison the wasps.
TODD	Yes, I think all the wasps have got to go.
HARPER	I was outside yesterday on the edge of the wood when a shadow came over and it was a cloud of butterflies, and they came down just beyond me and the trees and bushes were red with them. Two of them clung to my arm, I was terrified, one of them got in my hair, I managed to squash them.
TODD	I haven't had a problem with butterflies.
HARPER	They can cover your face. The Romans used to commit suicide with gold leaf, just flip it down their throat and it covered their windpipe, I think of that with butterflies.
TODD	I was passing an orchard, there were horses standing under the trees, and suddenly wasps attacked them out of the plums. There were the horses galloping by screaming with their heads made of wasp. I wish she'd wake up.
HARPER	We don't know how long she'd been walking.
TODD	She was right to come.
HARPER	You don't go walking off in the middle of a war.

TODD	You do if you're escaping.
HARPER	We don't know that she was escaping.
TODD	She was getting to a place of safety to regroup.
HARPER	Is this a place of safety?
TODD	Relatively, yes of course it is. Everyone thinks it's just a house.
HARPER	The cats have come in on the side of the French.
TODD	I never liked cats, they smell, they scratch, they only like you because you feed them, they bite, I used to have a cat that would suddenly just take some bit of you in its mouth.
HARPER	Did you know they've been killing babies?
TODD	Where's that?
HARPER	In China. They jump in the cots when nobody's looking.
TODD	But some cats are still ok.
HARPER	I don't think so.
TODD	I know a cat up the road.
HARPER	No, you must be careful of that.
TODD	But we're not exactly on the other side from the French. It's not as if they're the Moroccans and the ants.

HARPER   It's not as if they're the Canadians, the
          Venezuelans and the mosquitoes.

TODD   It's not as if they're the engineers, the chefs,
          the children under five, the musicians.

HARPER   The car salesmen.

TODD   Portuguese car salesmen.

HARPER   Russian swimmers.

TODD   Thai butchers.

HARPER   Latvian dentists.

TODD   No, the Latvian dentists have been doing
          good work in Cuba. They've a house outside
          Havana.

HARPER   But Latvia has been sending pigs to Sweden.
          The dentists are linked to international
          dentistry and that's where their loyalty lies,
          with dentists in Dar-es-Salaam.

TODD   We don't argue about Dar-es-Salaam.

HARPER   You would attempt to justify the massacre in
          Dar-es-Salaam?

          She's come here because you're here on leave
          and if anyone finds out I'll be held
          responsible.

TODD   It's only till tomorrow. I'll wake her up. I'll
          give her a few more minutes.

HARPER   Did you see the programme about
          crocodiles?

TODD   Yes but crocodiles, the way they look after
            the baby crocodiles and carry them down to
            the water in their mouths.

HARPER   Don't you think everyone helps their own
            children?

TODD   I'm just saying I wouldn't be sorry if the
            crocodiles were on one of the sides we have
            alliances with. They're unstoppable, come
            on.

HARPER   Crocodiles are evil and it is always right to be
            opposed to crocodiles. Their skin, their teeth,
            the foul smell of their mouths from the dead
            meat. Crocodiles wait till zebras are crossing
            the river and bite the weak ones with those
            jaws and pull them down. Crocodiles
            invade villages at night and take children out
            of their beds. A crocodile will carry a dozen
            heads back to the river, tenderly like it carries
            its young, and put them in the water where
            they bob about as trophies till they rot.

TODD   I'm just saying we could use that.

HARPER   And the fluffy little darling waterbirds, the
            smallest one left behind squeaking wait for
            me, wait for me. And their mother who
            would give her life to save them.

TODD   Do we include mallards in this?

HARPER   Mallards are not a good waterbird. They
            commit rape, and they're on the side of the
            elephants and the Koreans. But crocodiles
            are always in the wrong.

TODD   Do you think I should wake her up or let her
            sleep? We won't get any time together.

HARPER   You agree with me about the crocodiles?

TODD   What's the matter? you don't know whose
                side I'm on?

HARPER   I don't know what you think.

TODD   I think what we all think.

HARPER   Take deer.

TODD   You mean sweet little bambis?

HARPER   You mean that ironically?

TODD   I mean it sarcastically.

HARPER   Because they burst out of parks and storm
                down from mountains and terrorise shopping
                malls. If the does run away when you shoot
                they run into somebody else and trample
                them with their vicious little shining hooves,
                the fawns get under the feet of shoppers and
                send them crashing down escalators, the
                young bucks charge the plate glass windows –

TODD   I know to hate deer.

HARPER   and the old ones, do you know how heavy
                their antlers are or how sharp the prongs are
                when they twist into teenagers running down
                the street?

TODD   Yes I do know that.

                He lifts his shirt and shows a scar.

HARPER   Was that a deer?

TODD   In fact it was a bear. I don't like being
                doubted.

HARPER	It was when the elephants went over to the Dutch, I'd always trusted elephants.
TODD	I've shot cattle and children in Ethiopia. I've gassed mixed troops of Spanish, computer programmers and dogs. I've torn starlings apart with my bare hands. And I liked doing it with my bare hands. So don't suggest I'm not reliable.
HARPER	I'm not saying you can't kill.
TODD	And I know it's not all about excitement. I've done boring jobs. I've worked in abattoirs stunning pigs and musicians and by the end of the day your back aches and all you can see when you shut your eyes is people hanging upside down by their feet.
HARPER	So you'd say the deer are vicious?
TODD	We've been over that.
HARPER	If a hungry deer came into the yard you wouldn't feed it?
TODD	Of course not.
HARPER	I don't understand that because the deer are with us. They have been for three weeks.
TODD	I didn't know. You said yourself.
HARPER	Their natural goodness has come through. You can see it in their soft brown eyes.
TODD	That's good news.
HARPER	You hate the deer. You admire the crocodiles.
TODD	I've lost touch because I'm tired.

HARPER   You must leave.

TODD   I'm your family.

HARPER   Do you think I sleep?

              JOAN *comes in and walks into* TODD*'s arms.*

              You can't stay here, they'll be after you. What
              are you going to say when you go back, you
              ran off to spend a day with your husband?
              Everyone has people they love they'd like to
              see or anyway people they'd rather see than
              lie in a hollow waiting to be bitten by ants.
              Are you not going back at all because if
              you're not you might as well shoot me now.
              Did anyone see you leave? which way did you
              come? were you followed? There are ospreys
              here who will have seen you arrive. And
              you're risking your life for you don't know
              what because he says things that aren't right.
              Don't you care? Maybe you don't know right
              from wrong yourself, what do I know about
              you after two years, I'd like to be glad to see
              you but how can I?

JOAN   Of course birds saw me, everyone saw me
              walking along but nobody knew why, I could
              have been on a mission, everyone's moving
              about and no one knows why, and in fact I
              killed two cats and a child under five so it
              wasn't that different from a mission, and I
              don't see why I can't have one day and then
              go back, I'll go on to the end after this. It
              wasn't so much the birds I was frightened of,
              it was the weather, the weather here's on the
              side of the Japanese. There were
              thunderstorms all through the mountains, I
              went through towns I hadn't been before.
              The rats are bleeding out of their mouths

and ears, which is good, and so were the girls
by the side of the road. It was tiring there
because everything's been recruited, there
were piles of bodies and if you stopped to
find out there was one killed by coffee or one
killed by pins, they were killed by heroin,
petrol, chainsaws, hairspray, bleach,
foxgloves, the smell of smoke was where we
were burning the grass that wouldn't serve.
The Bolivians are working with gravity, that's
a secret so as not to spread alarm. But we're
getting further with noise and there's
thousands dead of light in Madagascar.
Who's going to mobilise darkness and
silence? that's what I wondered in the night.
By the third day I could hardly walk but I got
down to the river. There was a camp of
Chilean soldiers upstream but they hadn't
seen me and fourteen black and white cows
downstream having a drink so I knew I'd
have to go straight across. But I didn't know
whose side the river was on, it might help me
swim or it might drown me. In the middle
the current was running much faster, the
water was brown, I didn't know if that meant
anything. I stood on the bank a long time.
But I knew it was my only way of getting
here so at last I put one foot in the river. It
was very cold but so far that was all. When
you've just stepped in you can't tell what's
going to happen. The water laps round your
ankles in any case.

A NUMBER

A Number was first performed at the Royal Court Theatre Downstairs, London, on 23 September 2002, with the following cast:

Daniel Craig
Michael Gambon

Director   Stephen Daldry
Designer   Ian MacNeil
Lighting Designer   Rick Fisher
Sound Designer   Ian Dickinson

The play received its American premiere at the New York Theatre Workshop, on 16 November 2004, directed by James Macdonald, and performed by Sam Shepard and Dallas Roberts.

The play was filmed for television by HBO and the BBC for transmission in 2008, directed by James Macdonald, and performed by Tom Wilkinson and Rhys Ifans.

Characters

SALTER, *a man in his early sixties*

BERNARD, *his son, forty*

BERNARD, *his son, thirty-five*

MICHAEL BLACK, *his son, thirty-five*

The play is for two actors. One plays Salter, the other his sons.

The scene is the same throughout, it's where Salter lives.

1.

SALTER, *a man in his early sixties and his son* BERNARD (B2), *thirty-five.*

B2	A number
SALTER	you mean
B2	a number of them, of us, a considerable
SALTER	say
B2	ten, twenty
SALTER	didn't you ask?
B2	I got the impression
SALTER	why didn't you ask?
B2	I didn't think of asking.
SALTER	I can't think why not, it seems to me it would be the first thing you'd want to know, how far has this thing gone, how many of these things are there?
B2	Good, so if it ever happens to you
SALTER	no you're right
B2	no it was stupid, it was shock, I'd known for a week before I went to the hospital but it was still
SALTER	it is, I am, the shocking thing is that there *are* these, not how many but at all
B2	even one

SALTER	exactly, even one, a twin would be a shock
B2	a twin would be a surprise but a number
SALTER	a number any number is a shock.
B2	You said things, these things
SALTER	I said?
B2	you called them things. I think we'll find they're people.
SALTER	Yes of course they are, they are of course.
B2	Because I'm one.
SALTER	No.
B2	Yes. Why not? Yes.
SALTER	Because they're copies
B2	copies? they're not
SALTER	copies of you which some mad scientist has illegally
B2	how do you know that?
SALTER	I don't but
B2	what if someone else is the one, the first one, the real one and I'm
SALTER	no because
B2	not that I'm *not* real which is why I'm saying they're not things, don't call them
SALTER	just wait, because I'm your father.
B2	You know that?
SALTER	Of course.
B2	It was all a normal, everything, birth

SALTER	you think I wouldn't know if I wasn't your father?
B2	Yes of course I was just for a moment there, but they are all still people like twins are all, quins are all
SALTER	yes I'm sorry
B2	we just happen to have identical be identical identical genetic
SALTER	sorry I said things, I didn't mean anything by that, it just
B2	no forget it, it's nothing, it's
SALTER	because of course for me you're the
B2	yes I know what you meant, I just, because of course I want them to be things, I do think they're things, I don't think they're, of course I *do* think they're them just as much as I'm me but I. I don't know what I think, I feel terrible.
SALTER	I wonder if we can sue.
B2	Sue? who?
SALTER	Them, whoever did it. Who did you see?
B2	Just some young, I don't know, younger than me.
SALTER	So who did it?
B2	He's dead, he was some old and they've just found the records and they've traced
SALTER	so we sue the hospital.
B2	Maybe. Maybe we can.
SALTER	Because they've taken your cells

B2	but when how did they?
SALTER	when you were born maybe or later you broke your leg when you were two you were in the hospital, some hairs or scrapings of your skin
B2	but they didn't damage
SALTER	but it's you, part of you, the value
B2	the value of those people
SALTER	yes
B2	and what is the value of
SALTER	there you are, who knows, priceless, and they belong
B2	no
SALTER	they belong to you, they should belong to you, they're made from your
B2	they should
SALTER	they've been stolen from you and you should get your rights
B2	but is it
SALTER	what? is it money? is it something you can put a figure on? put a figure on it.
B2	This is purely
SALTER	yes
B2	suppose each person was worth ten thousand pounds
SALTER	a hundred
B2	a hundred thousand?

SALTER	they've taken a person away from you
B2	times the number of people
SALTER	which we don't know
B2	but a number a fairly large say anyway ten
SALTER	a million is the least you should take, I think it's more like half a million each person because what they've done they've damaged your uniqueness, weakened your identity, so we're looking at five million for a start.
B2	Maybe.
SALTER	Yes, because how dare they?
B2	We'd need to be able to prove
SALTER	we prove you're genetically my son genetically and then
B2	because there's no doubt
SALTER	no doubt at all. I suppose you didn't see one?
B2	One what? of them?
SALTER	of these people
B2	no I think they'd keep us apart wouldn't they so we don't spoil like contaminate the crime scene so you don't tell each other I have nightmares oh come to think of it I have nightmares and he might have said no if he was asked in the first place
SALTER	because they need to find out
B2	yes how much we're the same, not just how tall we are or do we get asthma but what do you call your dog, why did you leave your wife you don't even know the answer to these questions.

SALTER   So you didn't suddenly suddenly see

B2   what suddenly see myself coming round the
                corner

SALTER   because that could be

B2   like seeing yourself on the camera in a shop
                or you hear yourself on the answering
                machine and you think god is that what I

SALTER   but more than that, it'd be it'd be

B2   don't they say you die if you meet yourself?

SALTER   walk round the corner and see yourself you
                could get a heart attack. Because if that's me
                over there who am I?

B2   Yes but it's not me over there

SALTER   no I know

B2   it's like having a twin that's all it's just

SALTER   I know what it is.

B2   I think I'd like to meet one. It's an adventure
                isn't it and you're part of science. I wouldn't
                be frightened to meet any number.

SALTER   I don't know.

B2   They're all your sons.

SALTER   I don't want a number of sons, thank you,
                you're plenty, I'm fine.

B2   Maybe after they've found everything out
                they'll let us meet. They'll have a party for
                us, we can

SALTER   I'm not going to drink with those doctors.
                But maybe you're right you're right, take it in
                a positive spirit.

B2	There is a thing
SALTER	what's that?
B2	a thing that puzzles me a little
SALTER	what's that?
B2	I did get the impression and I know I may be wrong because maybe I was in shock but I got the impression there was this batch and we were all in it. I was in it.
SALTER	No because you're my son.
B2	No but we were all
SALTER	I explained already
B2	but I wasn't being quite open with you because I'm confused because it's a shock but I want to know what happened
SALTER	they stole
B2	no but what happened
SALTER	I don't
B2	because they said that none of us was the original.
SALTER	They said that?
B2	I think
SALTER	I think you're mistaken because you're confused
B2	you think
SALTER	you need to get back to them
B2	well I'll do that. But I think that's what they meant
SALTER	it's not what they meant

B2	ok. But that's my impression, that none of us is the original.
SALTER	Then who? do they know?
B2	they're not saying, they just say we were all
SALTER	they're not saying?
B2	so if I was your son the original would be your son too which is nonsense so
SALTER	does that follow?
B2	so please if you're not my father that's fine. If you couldn't have children or my mother, and you did in vitro or I don't know what you did I really think you should tell me.
SALTER	Yes, that's what it was.
B2	That's all right.
SALTER	Yes I know.
B2	Thank you for telling me.
SALTER	Yes.
B2	It's better to know.
SALTER	Yes.
B2	So don't be upset.
SALTER	No.
B2	You are though
SALTER	Well.
B2	I'm fine about it. I'm not quite sure what I'm fine about. There was some other person this original some baby or cluster or and there were a number a number of us made somehow and you were one of the people who acquired, something like that.

SALTER	It wasn't
B2	don't worry
SALTER	because the thing is you see that isn't what happened. I am your father, it was by an artificial the forefront of science but I am genetically.
B2	That's great.
SALTER	Yes.
B2	So I know the truth and you're still my father and that's fine.
SALTER	Yes.
B2	So what about this original? I don't quite I don't
SALTER	There was someone.
B2	There was what kind of someone?
SALTER	There was a son.
B2	A son of yours?
SALTER	Yes.
B2	So when was that?
SALTER	That was some time earlier.
B2	Some time before I was born there was
SALTER	another son, yes, a first
B2	who what, who died
SALTER	who died, yes
B2	and you wanted to replace him
SALTER	I wanted
B2	instead of just having another child you wanted

SALTER	because your mother was dead too
B2	but she died when I was born, I thought she
SALTER	well I'm telling you what happened.
B2	So what happened?
SALTER	So they'd been killed in a carcrash and
B2	my mother and this
SALTER	carcrash
B2	when was this? how old was the child, was he
SALTER	four, he was four
B2	and you wanted him back
SALTER	yes
B2	so I'm just him over again.
SALTER	No but you are you because that's who you are but I wanted one just the same because that seemed to me the most perfect
B2	but another child might have been better
SALTER	no I wanted the same
B2	but I'm not him
SALTER	no but you're just the way I wanted
B2	but I could have been a different person not like him I
SALTER	how could you? if I'd had a different child that wouldn't be you, would it. You're this one.
B2	I'm just a copy. I'm not the real one.
SALTER	You're the only one.

B2	What do you mean only, there's all the others, there's
SALTER	but I didn't know that, that wasn't part of the deal. They were meant to make one of you not a whole number, they stole that, we'll deal with, it's something for lawyers. But you're what I wanted, you're the one.
B2	Did you give me the same name as him?
SALTER	Does it make it worse?
B2	Probably.

2.

SALTER *and his other son* BERNARD (B1), *forty.*

SALTER   So they stole – don't look at me – they stole
            your genetic material and

B1   no

SALTER   they're the ones you want to

B1   no

SALTER   because what ten twenty twenty copies of
            you walking round the streets

B1   no

SALTER   which was nothing to do with me whatsoever
            and I think you and I should be united on
            this.

B1   Let me look at you.

SALTER   You've been looking at me all the

B1   let me look at you.

SALTER   Bit older.

B1   No because your father's not young when
            you're small is he, he's not any age, he's more
            a power. He's a dark dark power which is
            why my heart, people pay trainers to get it
            up to this speed, but is it because my body
            recognises or because I'm told? because if I'd
            seen you in the street I don't think I'd've
            stopped and shouted Daddy. But you'd've
            known me wouldn't you. Unless you thought
            I was one of the others.

SALTER	It's a long time.
B1	Can we talk about what you did?
SALTER	Yes of course. I'm not sure where what
B1	about you sent me away and had this other one made from some bit of my body some
SALTER	it didn't hurt you
B1	what bit
SALTER	I don't know what
B1	not a limb, they clearly didn't take a limb like a starfish and grow
SALTER	a speck
B1	or half of me chopped through like a worm and grow the other
SALTER	a scraping cells a speck a speck
B1	a speck yes because we're talking that microscope world of giant blobs and globs
SALTER	that's all
B1	and they take this painless scrape this specky little cells of me and kept that and you threw the rest of me away
SALTER	no
B1	and had a new one made
SALTER	no
B1	yes
SALTER	yes
B1	yes
SALTER	yes of course, you know I did, I'm not attempting to deny, I thought it was the best

	thing to do, it seemed a brilliant it was the only
B1	brilliant?
SALTER	it seemed
B1	to get rid
SALTER	it wasn't perfect. It was the best I could do, I wasn't very I was I was always and it's a blur to be honest but it was I promise you the best
B1	and this copy they grew of me, that worked out all right?
SALTER	There were failures of course, inevitable
B1	dead ones
SALTER	in the test tubes the dishes, I was told they didn't all
B1	but they finally got a satisfactory a bouncing
SALTER	yes but they lied to me because they didn't tell me
B1	in a cradle
SALTER	all those others, they stole
B1	and he looked just like me did he indistinguishable from
SALTER	yes
B1	so it worked out very well. And this son lives and breathes?
SALTER	yes
B1	talks and fucks? eats and walks? swims and dreams and exists somewhere right now yes does he? exist now?

SALTER	yes
B1	still exists
SALTER	yes of course
B1	happily?
SALTER	well mostly you could say
B1	as happily as most people?
SALTER	yes I think
B1	because most people are happy I read in the paper. Did it cost a lot of money?
SALTER	the procedure? to get?
B1	the baby
SALTER	yes.
B1	Were we rich?
SALTER	Not rich.
B1	No, I don't remember anything rich. A lot of dust under the bed those heaps of fluff you get don't you if you look if you go under there and lie in it.
SALTER	No, we weren't. But I managed. I was spending less.
B1	You made an effort.
SALTER	I did and for that money you'd think I'd get exclusive
B1	they ripped you off
SALTER	because one one was the deal and they
B1	what do you expect?

SALTER	from you too they it's you they, just so they can do some scientific some research some do you get asthma do you have a dog what do you call it do you
B1	Who did you think it was at the door? did you think it was one of the others or your son or
SALTER	I don't know the others
B1	you know your son
SALTER	I know
B1	your son the new
SALTER	yes of course
B1	you know him
SALTER	yes I wouldn't think he was you, no.
B1	You wouldn't think it was him having a bad day.
SALTER	You look very well.
B1	But it could have been one of the others?
SALTER	Yes because that's what I was thinking about, how could the doctors, I think there's money to be made out of this.
B1	I've not been lucky with dogs. I had this black and tan bitch wouldn't do what it's told, useless. Before that I had a lurcher they need too much running about. Then a friend of mine went inside could I look after, battle from day one with that dog, rottweiler pit bull I had to throw a chair, you could hit it with a belt it kept coming back. I'd keep it shut up in the other room and it barks so you have to hit it, I was glad when it bit a girl went to pat it and straight off to the vet, get

rid of this one it's a bastard. My friend
wasn't pleased but he shouldn't have gone in
the postoffice.

SALTER   No that's right. I've never wanted a dog.

B1   Don't patronise me

SALTER   I'm not I'm not

B1   you don't know what you're doing

SALTER   I just

B1   because you go in a pub someone throws his
beer in your face you're supposed to say
sorry, he only had three stitches I'm a very
restrained person. Because this minute we sit
here there's somebody a lot of them but think
of one on the electric bedsprings or water
poured down his throat and jump on his
stomach. There's a lot of wicked people. So
that's why. And you see them all around you.
You go down the street and you see their
faces and you think you don't fool me I know
what you're capable of. So don't start
anything.

SALTER   I think what we need is a good solicitor.

B1   What I like about a dog it stops people
getting after you, they're not going to come
round in the night. But they make the place
stink because I might want to stay out a few
days and when I get back I might want to
stay in a few days and a dog can become a
tyrant to you.

Silence.

Hello daddy daddy daddy, daddy hello.

SALTER   Nobody regrets more than me the completely
unforeseen unforeseeable which isn't my fault
and does make it more upsetting but what I

did did seem at the time the only and also it's
a tribute, I could have had a different one, a
new child altogether that's what most people
but I wanted you again because I thought
you were the best.

B1   It wasn't me again.

SALTER   No but the same basic the same raw
materials because they were perfect. You
were the most beautiful baby everyone said.
As a child too you were very pretty, very
pretty child.

B1   You know when I used to be shouting.

SALTER   No.

B1   When I was there in the dark. I'd be
shouting.

SALTER   No.

B1   Yes, I'd be shouting dad dad

SALTER   Was this some time you had a bad dream or?

B1   shouting on and on

SALTER   I don't think I

B1   shouting and shouting

SALTER   no

B1   and you never came, nobody ever came

SALTER   so was this after your mum

B1   after my mum was dead this was after

SALTER   because you were very little when she

B1   yes because I can only remember

SALTER   you were maybe two when she

B1   and I remember her sitting there, she was
there

SALTER	you remember so early?
B1	she'd be there but she wouldn't help stop anything
SALTER	I'm surprised
B1	so when I was shouting what I want to know
SALTER	but when was this
B1	I want to know if you could hear me or not because I never knew were you hearing me and not coming or could you not hear me and if I shouted loud enough you'd come
SALTER	I can't have heard you, no
B1	or maybe there was no one there at all and you'd gone out so no matter how hard I shouted there was no one there
SALTER	no that wouldn't have
B1	so then I'd stop shouting but it was worse
SALTER	because I hardly ever
B1	and I didn't dare get out of bed to go and see
SALTER	I don't think this can have
B1	because if there was nobody there that would be terrifying and if you were there that might be worse but it's something I wonder
SALTER	no
B1	could you hear me shouting?
SALTER	no I don't
B1	no
SALTER	no I don't think this happened in quite the
B1	what?

SALTER	because I'd
B1	again and again and again, every night I'd be
SALTER	no
B1	so you didn't hear?
SALTER	no but you can't have
B1	yes I was shouting, are you telling me you didn't
SALTER	no of course I didn't
B1	you didn't
SALTER	no
B1	you weren't sitting there listening to me shouting
SALTER	no
B1	you weren't out
SALTER	no
B1	so I needed to shout louder.
SALTER	Of course sometimes everyone who's had children will tell you sometimes you put them to bed and they want another story and you say goodnight now and go away and they call out once or twice and you say no go to sleep now and they might call out again and they go to sleep.
B1	The other one. Your son. My brother is he? my little twin.
SALTER	Yes.
B1	Has he got a child?
SALTER	No.

B1   Because if he had I'd kill it.

SALTER   No, he hasn't got one.

B1   So when you opened the door you didn't
                  recognise me.

SALTER   No because

B1   Do you recognise me now?

SALTER   I know it's you.

B1   No but look at me.

SALTER   I have. I am.

B1   No, look in my eyes. No, keep looking. Look.

3.

SALTER *and* BERNARD (B2).

B2	Not like me at all
SALTER	not like
B2	well like like but not identical not
SALTER	not identical no not
B2	because what struck me was how different
SALTER	yes I was struck
B2	you couldn't mistake
SALTER	no no not at all I knew at once it wasn't
B2	though of course he is older if I was older
SALTER	but even then you wouldn't
B2	I wouldn't be identical
SALTER	no no not at all no, you're a different
B2	just a bit like
SALTER	well bound to be a bit
B2	because for a start I'm not frightening.
SALTER	So what did he want did he
B2	no nothing really, not frightening not
SALTER	he didn't hit you?
B2	hit? god no, hit me? do you think?

SALTER	well he
B2	he could have done yes, no he shouted
SALTER	shouted
B1	shouted and rambled really, rambled he's not entirely
SALTER	no, well
B2	so that's what, his childhood, his life, his childhood
SALTER	all kinds of
B2	has made him a nutter really is what I think I mean not a nutter but he's
SALTER	yes yes I'm not, yes he probably is.
B2	He says all kinds of wild
SALTER	yes
B2	so you don't know what to believe.
SALTER	And how did it end up, are you on friendly
B2	friendly no
SALTER	not
B2	no no we ended up
SALTER	yes
B2	we ended as I mean to go on with me running away, I was glad we were meeting in a public place, if I'd been at home you can't run away in your own home and if we'd been at his I wonder if he'd have let me go he might put me in a cupboard not really, anyway yes I got up and left and I kept thinking had he followed me.

SALTER   As you mean to go on as in not seeing him
              any more

B2   as in leaving the country.

SALTER   For what for a week or two a holiday, I don't

B2   leaving, going on yes I don't know, going
              away, I don't want to be here.

SALTER   But when you come back he'll still

B2   so maybe I won't

SALTER   but that's, not come back, no that's

B2   I don't know I don't know don't ask me I
              don't know. I'm going, I don't know. I don't
              want to be anywhere near him.

SALTER   You think he might try to hurt you?

B2   Why? why do you keep

SALTER   I don't know. Is it that?

B2   It's partly that, it's also it's horrible, I don't
              feel myself and there's the others too, I don't
              want to see them I don't want them

SALTER   I thought you did.

B2   I thought I did, I might, if I go away
              by myself I might feel all right, I might feel –
              you can understand that.

SALTER   Yes, yes I can.

B2   Because there's this person who's identical to
              me

SALTER   he's not

B2   who's not identical, who's like

SALTER   not even very

B2	not very like but very something terrible which is exactly the same genetic person
SALTER	not the same person
B2	and I don't like it.
SALTER	I know. I'm sorry.
B2	I know you're sorry I'm not
SALTER	I know
B2	I'm not trying to make you say sorry
SALTER	I know, I just am
B2	I know
SALTER	I just am sorry.
B2	He said some things.
SALTER	Yes.
B2	There's a lot of things I don't, could you tell me what happened to my mother?
SALTER	She's dead.
B2	Yes.
SALTER	I told you she was dead.
B2	Yes but she didn't die when I was born and she didn't die with the first child in a carcrash because the first child's not dead he's walking round the streets at night giving me nightmares. Unless she did die in a carcrash?
SALTER	No.
B2	No.
SALTER	Your mother, the thing a thing about your mother was that she wasn't very happy, she

wasn't a very happy person at all, I don't
mean there were sometimes days she wasn't
happy or I did things that made her not
happy I did of course, she was always not
happy, often cheerful and

B2   she killed herself. How did she do that?

SALTER   She did it under a train under a tube train,
            she was one of those people when they say
            there has been a person under a train and
            the trains are delayed she was a person under
            a train.

B2   Were you with her?

SALTER   With her on the platform no, I was still *with*
            her more or less but not with her then no I
            was having a drink I think.

B2   And the boy?

SALTER   Do you know I don't remember where the
            boy was. I think he was at a friend's house,
            we had friends.

B2   And he was how old four?

SALTER   no no he was four later when I he was
            walking, about two just starting to talk

B2   he was four when you sent him

SALTER   that's right when his mother died he was two.

B2   So this was let me be clear this was before
            this was some years before I was born she
            died before

SALTER   yes

B2   so she was already always

SALTER   yes she was

B2	just so I'm clear. And then you and the boy you and your son
SALTER	we went on we just
B2	lived alone together
SALTER	yes
B2	you were bringing him up
SALTER	yes
B2	the best you could
SALTER	I
B2	until
SALTER	and my best wasn't very but I had my moments, don't think, I did cook meals now and then and read a story I'm sure I can remember a particularly boring and badly written little book about an elephant at sea. But I could have managed better.
B2	Yes he said something about it
SALTER	he said
B2	yes
SALTER	yes of course he did yes. I know I could have managed better because I did with you because I stopped, shut myself away, gave it all up came off it all while I waited for you and I think we may even have had that same book, maybe it's you I remember reading it to, do you remember it at all? it had an elephant in red trousers.
B2	No I don't think
SALTER	no it was terrible, we had far better books we had

B2   Maybe he shouldn't blame you, maybe it was
              a genetic, could you help drinking we don't
              know or drugs at the time philosophically as I
              understand it it wasn't viewed as not like now
              when our understanding's different and
              would a different person genetically different
              person not have been so been so vulnerable
              because there could always be some genetic
              addictive and then again someone with the
              same genetic exactly the same but at a
              different time a different cultural and of
              course all the personal all kinds of what
              happened in your own life your childhood or
              things all kind of because suppose you'd had
              a brother with identical an identical twin say
              but separated at birth so you had entirely
              different early you see what I'm saying would
              he have done the same things who can say he
              might have been a very loving father and in
              fact of course you have that in you to be that
              because you were to me so it's a combination
              of very complicated and that's who you were
              so probably I shouldn't blame you.

SALTER   I'd rather you blamed me. I blame myself.

B2   I'm not saying you weren't horrible.

SALTER   Couldn't I not have been?

B2   Apparently not.

SALTER   If I'd tried harder.

B2   But someone like you couldn't have tried
              harder. What does it mean? If you'd tried
              harder you'd have been different from what
              you were like and you weren't you were

SALTER   but then later I

B2   later yes

SALTER	I did try that's what I did I started again I
B2	that's what
SALTER	I was good I tried to be good I was good to you
B2	that's what you were like
SALTER	I was good
B2	but I can't you can't I can't give you credit for that if I don't give you blame for the other it's what you did it's what happened
SALTER	but it felt
B2	it felt
SALTER	it felt as if I tried I deliberately
B2	of course it felt
SALTER	well then
B2	it feels it always it feels doesn't it inside that's just how we feel what we are and we don't know all these complicated we can't know what we're it's too complicated to disentangle all the causes and we feel this is me I freely and of course it's true who you are does freely not forced by someone else but who you are who you are itself forces or you'd be someone else wouldn't you?
SALTER	I did some bad things. I deserve to suffer. I did some better things. I'd like recognition.
B2	That's how everyone feels, certainly.
SALTER	He still blames me.
B2	There's a difference then.
SALTER	You remind me of him.

B2	I remind myself of him. We both hate you.
SALTER	I thought you
B2	I don't blame you it's not your fault but what you've been like what you're like I can't help it.
SALTER	Yes of course.
B2	Except what he feels as hate and what I feel as hate are completely different because what you did to him and what you did to me are different things.
SALTER	I was nice to you.
B2	Yes you were.
SALTER	You don't have to go away. Not for long.
B2	It might make me feel better.
SALTER	I love you.
B2	That's something else you can't help.
SALTER	That's all right. That's all right.
B2	Also I'm afraid he'll kill me.

4.

SALTER *and* BERNARD (B1).

SALTER	So what kind of a place was it? was it
B1	the place
SALTER	he was in a hotel was he or
B1	no
SALTER	I thought he was in a hotel. So where was he?
B1	what?
SALTER	I'm trying to get a picture.
B1	Does it matter?
SALTER	It won't bring him back no obviously but I'd like I'd like you can't help feeling curious you want to get at it and you're blocked in all directions, your son dies you want his body, you want to know where his body last was when he was alive, you can't help
B1	He had a room.
SALTER	In somebody's house, renting
B1	some small you know how the locals when you arrive, just a room not breakfast you'd go out for a coffee.
SALTER	So was it some pretty on a harbour front or
B1	no
SALTER	thinking of him on holiday

B1   in a street just a side

SALTER   but of course it wasn't a holiday he was
                      hiding he thought he was hiding. Did you go
                      inside the room?

B1   Just a small room, rather dark, one window
                      and the shutters

SALTER   not very tidy I expect

B1   that's right, not tidy the bed not made,
                      couple of books, bag on the floor with
                      clothes half out of it

SALTER   did he scream?

B1   and you know what he's like, not tidy, am I
                      tidy you don't know do you but you'd guess
                      not wouldn't you but you'd be wrong there
                      because I'm meticulous.

SALTER   What I want to know is how you actually,
                      what you, how you got him to go off to some
                      remote because that's what I'm imagining,
                      you don't shoot the lodger without the
                      landlady hearing, I don't know if you did
                      shoot I don't know why I say shoot you could
                      have had a knife you could have strangled, I
                      can't think he would have gone off with you
                      because he was frightened which is why but
                      perhaps you talked you made him feel or did
                      you follow him or lie in wait in some dark?
                      and I don't know how you found him there
                      did you follow him from his house when he
                      left or follow him from here last time he?

B1   I didn't need to tell you it had happened

SALTER   but you did so naturally I want to

B1   and I'm wishing I hadn't

SALTER   no I'm glad

B1	and I'm not telling you
SALTER	because I won't tell anyone
B1	and there's nothing more to be said.
SALTER	What about the others? or is he the only one you hated because I loved him, I don't love the others, you and I have got common cause against the others don't forget, I'm still hoping we'll make our fortunes there. I'm going to talk to a solicitor, I've been too busy not busy but it's been like a storm going on I don't know what's gone on, it's not been very long ago it all started. You're not going to be a serial, wipe them all out so you're the only, back like it was at the start I'd understand that. If they do catch up with you, I'm sure they won't I'm sure you know what you're, if they do we'll tell them it was me it was my fault anyway you look at it. Don't you agree, don't you feel that? Don't stop talking to me. It wasn't his fault, you should have killed me, it's my fault you. Perhaps you're going to kill me, is that why you've stopped talking? Shall I kill myself? I'd do that for you if you like, would you like that?

I'll tell you a thought, I could have killed you and I didn't. I may have done terrible things but I didn't kill you. I could have killed you and had another son, made one the same like I did or start again have a different one get married again and I didn't, I spared you though you were this disgusting thing by then anyone in their right mind would have squashed you but I remembered what you'd been like at the beginning and I spared you, I didn't want a different one, I wanted that again because you were perfect just like that and I loved you.

You know you asked me when you used to
shout in the night. Sometimes I was there, I'd
sit and listen to you or I'd not be in any
condition to hear you I'd just be sitting.
Sometimes I'd go out and leave you. I don't
think you got out of bed, did you get out of
bed, because you'd be frightened what I'd do
to you so it was all right to go out. That was
just a short period you used to shout, you
grew out of that, you got so you'd rather not
see me, you wanted to be left alone in the
night, you wouldn't want me to come any
more. You'd nearly stopped speaking do you
remember that? not speaking not eating I
tried to make you. I'd put you in the
cupboard do you remember? or I'd look for
you everywhere and I'd think you'd got away
and I'd find you under the bed. You liked it
there I'd put your dinner under for you. But
it got worse do you remember? There was
nobody but us. One day I cleaned you up
and said take him into care. You didn't look
too bad and they took you away. My darling.
Do you remember that? Do you remember
that day because I don't remember it you
know. The whole thing is very vague to me.
It's two years I remember almost nothing
about but you must remember things and
when you're that age two years is much
longer, it wasn't very long to me, it was one
long night out. Can you tell me anything you
remember? the day you left? can you tell me
things I did I might have forgotten?

B1   When I was following him there was a time I
was getting on the same train and he looked
round, I thought he was looking right at me
but he didn't see me. I got on the train and
went with him all the way.

SALTER   Yes? yes?

5.

SALTER *and* MICHAEL BLACK, *his son, thirty-five.*

MICHAEL	Have you met the others?
SALTER	You're the first.
MICHAEL	Are you going to meet us all?
SALTER	I thought I'd start.
MICHAEL	I'm sure everyone will be pleased to meet you. I know I am.
SALTER	I'm sorry to stare.
MICHAEL	No, please, I can see it must be. Do I look like?
SALTER	Yes of course
MICHAEL	of course, I meant
SALTER	no no I didn't mean
MICHAEL	I suppose I meant how
SALTER	because of course you don't, you don't, not exactly
MICHAEL	no of course
SALTER	I wouldn't mistake
MICHAEL	no
SALTER	or I might at a casual
MICHAEL	of course
SALTER	but not if I really look

MICHAEL   no

SALTER   no

MICHAEL   because?

SALTER   because of the eyes. You don't look at me in the same way.

MICHAEL   I'm looking at someone I don't know of course.

SALTER   Maybe you could tell me a little

MICHAEL   about myself

SALTER   if you don't mind

MICHAEL   no of course, it's where to, you already know I'm a teacher, mathematics, you know I'm married, three children did I tell you that

SALTER   yes but you didn't

MICHAEL   boy and girl twelve and eight and now a baby well eighteen months so she's walking and beginning to talk, I don't have any photographs on me I didn't think, there's no need for photographs is there if you see someone all the time so

SALTER   are you happy?

MICHAEL   what now? or in general? Yes I think I am, I don't think about it, I am. The job gets me down sometimes. The world's a mess of course. But you can't help, a sunny morning, leaves turning, off to the park with the baby, you can't help feeling wonderful can you?

SALTER   Can't you?

MICHAEL   Well that's how I seem to be.

SALTER   Tell me. Forgive me

MICHAEL   no go on

SALTER   tell me something about yourself that's really
              specific to you, something really important

MICHAEL   what sort of?

SALTER   anything

MICHAEL   it's hard to

SALTER   yes.

MICHAEL   Well here's something I find fascinating, there
              are these people who used to live in holes in
              the ground, with all tunnels and
              underground chambers and sometimes you'd
              have a chamber you'd get to it through a
              labyrinth of passages and the ceiling got
              lower and lower so you had to go on your
              hands and knees and then wriggle on your
              stomach and you'd get through to this
              chamber deep deep down that had a hole
              like a chimney like a well a hole all the way
              up to the sky so you could sit in this chamber
              this room this cave whatever and look up at a
              little circle of sky going past overhead. And
              when somebody died they'd hollow out more
              little rooms so they weren't buried
              underneath you they were buried in the walls
              beside you. And maybe sometimes they
              walled people up alive in there, it's possible
              because of how the remains were contorted
              but either way of course they're dead by now
              and very soon after they went in of course.
              And

SALTER   I don't think this is what I'm looking for

MICHAEL   oh, how, sorry

SALTER   because what you're telling me is about
              something else and I was hoping for
              something about you

MICHAEL   I don't quite

SALTER   I'm sorry I don't know I was hoping

MICHAEL   you want what my beliefs, politics how I feel
                 about war for instance is that? I dislike war,
                 I'm not at all happy when people say we're
                 doing a lot of good with our bombing, I'm
                 never very comfortable with that. War's one
                 of those things, don't you think, where
                 everyone always thinks they're in the right
                 have you noticed that? Nobody ever says
                 we're the bad guys, we're going to beat shit
                 out of the good guys. What do you think?

SALTER   I was hoping I don't know something more
                 personal something from deep inside your
                 life. If that's not intrusive.

MICHAEL   Maybe what maybe my wife's ears?

SALTER   Yes?

MICHAEL   Because last night we were watching the
                 news and I thought what beautiful and
                 slightly odd ears she's got, they're small but
                 with big lobes, big relative to the small ear,
                 and they're slightly pointy on top, like a
                 disney elf or little animal ears and they're
                 always there but you know how you suddenly
                 notice and noticing that, I mean the way I
                 love her, felt very felt what you said
                 something deep inside. Or the children
                 obviously, I could talk about, is this the sort
                 of thing?

SALTER   it's not quite

MICHAEL   no

SALTER   because you're just describing other people
                 or

MICHAEL   yes

SALTER   not yourself

MICHAEL   but it's people I love so

SALTER   it's not what I'm looking for. Because anyone
                could feel

MICHAEL   oh of course I'm not claiming

SALTER   I was somehow hoping

MICHAEL   yes

SALTER   further in

MICHAEL   yes

SALTER   just about yourself

MICHAEL   myself

SALTER   yes

MICHAEL   like maybe I'm lying in bed and it's
                comfortable and then it gets slightly not so
                comfortable and I move my legs or even turn
                over and then it's

SALTER   no

MICHAEL   no

SALTER   no that's

MICHAEL   yes that's something everyone

SALTER   yes

MICHAEL   well I don't know. I like blue socks. Banana
                icecream. Does that help you?

SALTER   Dogs?

MICHAEL   do I like

SALTER   dogs

MICHAEL   I'm ok with dogs. My daughter wants a puppy but I don't know. Is dogs the kind of thing?

SALTER   So tell me what did you feel when you found out?

MICHAEL   Fascinated.

SALTER   Not angry?

MICHAEL   No.

SALTER   Not frightened.

MICHAEL   No, what of?

SALTER   Your life, losing your life.

MICHAEL   I've still got my life.

SALTER   But there are things there are things that are what you are, I think you're avoiding

MICHAEL   yes perhaps

SALTER   because then you might be frightened

MICHAEL   I don't think

SALTER   or angry

MICHAEL   not really

SALTER   because what does it do what does it to you to everything if there are all these walking around, what it does to me what am I and it's not even me it happened to, so how you can just, you must think something about it.

MICHAEL   I think it's funny, I think it's delightful

SALTER   delightful?

MICHAEL   all these very similar people doing things like each other or a bit different or whatever we're doing, what a thrill for the mad old professor if he'd lived to see it, I do see the joy of it. I know you're not at all happy.

SALTER   I didn't feel I'd lost him when I sent him away because I had the second chance. And when the second one my son the second son was murdered it wasn't so bad as you'd think because it seemed fair. I was back with the first one.

MICHAEL   But now

SALTER   now he's killed himself

MICHAEL   now you feel

SALTER   now I've lost him, I've lost

MICHAEL   yes

SALTER   now I can't put it right any more. Because the second time round you see I slept very lightly with the door open.

MICHAEL   Is that the worst you did, not go in the night?

SALTER   No of course not.

MICHAEL   Like what?

SALTER   Things that are what I did that are not trivial like banana icecream nor unifuckingversal like turning over in bed.

MICHAEL   We've got ninety-nine per cent the same genes as any other person. We've got ninety per cent the same as a chimpanzee. We've got thirty percent the same as a lettuce. Does that cheer you up at all? I love about the lettuce. It makes me feel I belong.

SALTER   I miss him so much. I miss them both.

MICHAEL   There's nineteen more of us.

SALTER   That's not the same.

MICHAEL   No of course not. I was making a joke.

SALTER   And you're happy you say are you? you like
              your life?

MICHAEL   I do yes, sorry.

A DREAM PLAY

After Strindberg

Introduction

Is it a larder? Is it a fridge? Is it more fun, more vivid, or even
more true to what Strindberg meant, to update the larder door
which is just like the ones the Officer saw when he was a child?
A larder's where the food is, so does a fridge give us more
directly, without archaism, the promise of satisfaction of
appetite? And make it easier to see why the characters hope
that if they finally get the door open they'll find the meaning
of life inside? Or is it a silly idea and a modernism too far?

You don't of course consciously think all that, you think 'fridge'
and smile. I did this version for Katie Mitchell, who was already
planning to direct it at the National Theatre, and she had said
she welcomed anachronisms. So when the happy couple decide
to kill themselves because bliss doesn't last ('Life is wretched.
I pity mankind.'), I could write, 'People are so fucked up.'

There's a strand of the play that is about academia, and that's
where I've done the most updating. The university and its
bossy deans of theology, philosophy, medicine and law don't
have the power over us that they seemed to have over Strindberg.
Here a bishop, psychoanalyst, scientist and barrister are on the
committee of the inquiry looking into the opening of the door,
and the solicitor is refused not a doctorate but a knighthood.
Not a big change, and on the whole this version stays close to
the original.

What I've mostly done is tighten the dialogue and cut out a few
chunks. Strindberg lived in a far more Christian society than
ours, and his swipes at it look a bit unnecessary now, so I've
taken some of them out. Though, with a Christian prime
minister and an American president voted in by right-wing
Christians both calling us to fight evil, perhaps we should feel
as dominated by religion as Strindberg did. Still, we don't, so
I'm not restoring those cuts. I've cut references to the Flying
Dutchman and the Caliph Haroun; I've cut things that seemed
repetitive; sometimes I've cut bits that just seemed to me or
Katie not to work very well. And I've cut the meaning of life.

When it turns out there's nothing behind the fridge door, the daughter of the gods promises the writer she'll tell him the secret when they're alone. What she says may have seemed more original or daring when Strindberg wrote it, but seems a bit of an anticlimax to us. So in this version she whispers it to the writer and we never know what it is. But was telling us the meaning of life one of the main points of the play for Strindberg? I hope not. I do feel abashed at cutting another writer's work; directors have fewer qualms.

I said the version was close to the original but of course I've no idea what the original is as I don't know any Swedish. The very few translations I've done before have been from French or Latin, where I knew enough to see what the text was literally saying. I'd never wanted to work from a literal translation of a language I didn't know. To my surprise, the one I was given wasn't literally literal, the kind of thing I'd done for myself at first when translating Latin, with odd word order and odd words, but a translation, by Charlotte Barslund, which seemed to me as performable as the existing translations I'd looked at. So that for me is the original I've kept close to.

People who are looking at this text after seeing Katie Mitchell's production may or may not find considerable differences. Working as she has before, she and the actors may add other material or change the order of scenes, or they may end up very close to this text. I've put in Strindberg's stage directions, which are what Katie and designer Vicki Mortimer are starting from, rather than describing their solutions, since other productions may want to use this text and come up with their own versions of stage doors, caves and quarantine stations. When Strindberg was writing the play a castle was being built in Stockholm and grew over the trees, and the town was full of soldiers. The equivalent fast-growing buildings for us are office towers; a soldier means our current wars to us, not the romantic officer of the play; our city towers are full of businessmen. So we've gone for a tower, which works well both ways – prisoners are kept in towers – and for a while we went with a Banker instead of an Officer. Katie's staying with the Banker but I've gone back to the Officer for this text, feeling as with the stage directions that I shouldn't put too much of the production into it. I've kept the fridge though – if you're not happy with anachronism feel free to go back to the larder.

I'd read the play several times over the years, admired the way it moved, but never, I realise, taken in the detail. I was surprised by its tenderness. Since starting this version I've learned more about Strindberg than I knew before. I suppose I'd thought of him as misogynistic and depressive and mostly concerned with miserable relationships and disastrous families. All of which of course you can find in *A Dream Play*. I hadn't realised how political he was, that he was a hero to trade unionists, who made a detour in a parade to pass his window. When asked what mattered to him most he said, 'Disarmament.' He added the coal-miner scene (building workers here) after the play was finished, because there was a miners' strike in Stockholm.

I'm not sure how I'd feel if someone treated one of my plays the way I've treated Strindberg's, even though I hope I've made it clearer and not spoilt it. I wouldn't like it now, but perhaps when a play is over a hundred years old you should just be glad it's still being done. And it survives unharmed in Swedish. I'd like to think he'd be glad about this version. I'd like to make him smile. But maybe he'd say, 'Oh woe. Life is wretched.'

Caryl Churchill

Author's Note

As with his earlier dream play, *To Damascus*, the author has in this dream play sought to imitate the disjointed yet seemingly logical shape of a dream. Everything can happen, everything is possible and probable. Time and place do not exist; the imagination spins, weaving new patterns on a flimsy basis of reality: a mixture of memories, experiences, free associations, absurdities and improvisations.

The characters split, double, multiply, evaporate, condense, dissolve and merge. But one consciousness rules them all: the dreamer's; for him there are no secrets, no inconsistencies, no scruples and no laws. He does not judge or acquit, he merely relates; and, because a dream is usually painful rather than pleasant, a tone of melancholy and compassion for all living creatures permeates the rambling narrative. Sleep, the liberator, often feels like torture, but when the torment is at its worst, the moment of awakening comes and reconciles the sufferer with reality, which, regardless of how painful it might be, is at this very moment a joy compared to the agonies of dreaming.

August Strindberg

This version of *A Dream Play*, with additional material by Katie Mitchell and the company, was first performed in the Cottosloe auditorium of the National Theatre, London, on 15 February 2005 (previews from 4 February), with the following cast:

Mark Arends
Anastasia Hille
Kristin Hutchinson
Sean Jackson
Charlotte Roach
Dominic Rowan
Justin Salinger
Susie Trayling
Lucy Whybrow
Angus Wright

Director   Katie Mitchell
Designer   Vicki Mortimer
Lighting Designer   Chris Davey
Choreographer   Kate Flatt
Music Director and Arranger   Simon Allen
Sound Designer   Christopher Shutt

The play received its American premiere by Constellation Theatre Company at the Source Theatre, Washington DC, on 16 June 2007, directed by Allison Arkell Stockman.

Characters

AGNES, DAUGHTER OF THE GODS
GLAZIER

OFFICER
OFFICER'S FATHER AND MOTHER
LINA, THEIR MAID

STAGE DOOR KEEPER
BILLSTICKER
VICTORIA
SINGER
DANCER
PROMPTER
THEATRE PEOPLE
POLICEMEN

SOLICITOR
KRISTIN

RICH FAT SICK
QUARANTINE MASTER
WRITER
HE
SHE

MAIDS
EDITH
HER MOTHER
LIEUTENANT
ALICE
TEACHER
BOYS
NEWLYWEDS
BLIND MAN
TWO BUILDING WORKERS
LADY AND GENTLEMAN
CREW

CHAIR OF INQUIRY
BISHOP
PSYCHOANALYST
SCIENTIST
BARRISTER

1. Outside the Tower

Huge hollyhocks.

A tower with a flower bud on top.

AGNES *and* GLAZIER.

AGNES	Look how the tower's grown.
GLAZIER	What tower?
AGNES	It's twice the size it was last year.
GLAZIER	Yes of course, it must be the fertiliser.
AGNES	But shouldn't it be flowering by now?
GLAZIER	Can't you see the flower?
AGNES	Yes, yes, I see it. Do you know who lives in the tower?
GLAZIER	I do but I can't remember.
AGNES	I think it's a prisoner. And I think he's waiting for me to set him free. Let's go in.

2. Room inside the Tower

AGNES, GLAZIER, OFFICER.

OFFICER *is rocking his chair and hitting the table with his sword.*

AGNES	(*Takes the sword.*) Don't. Don't.

OFFICER	Please, Agnes, let me keep my sword.
AGNES	You're hacking the table. (*To* GLAZIER.) Go down to the tackroom and mend the window and I'll see you later.

GLAZIER *goes.*

You're a prisoner and I've come to set you free.

OFFICER	It's what I've been waiting for. But I wasn't sure you wanted to.
AGNES	Do you want to?
OFFICER	I don't know. I'll be miserable either way. It's terrible sitting here but it's going to be so painful being free. Agnes, I'd rather stay here if I can go on seeing you.
AGNES	What do you see?
OFFICER	I look at you and it's something to do with the stars and the smallest particles, you're somehow connected.
AGNES	But so are you.
OFFICER	Then why do I have to muck out the horses?
AGNES	To make you long to get away.
OFFICER	I do but it's such an effort.
AGNES	It's your duty to seek freedom in the light.
OFFICER	To be free is a duty?
AGNES	Your duty to life.
OFFICER	Life doesn't do its duty to me so why should I?

AGNES, OFFICER, FATHER, MOTHER.

MOTHER *is working on shirts at a table.*

FATHER *gives* MOTHER *a silk dress.*

FATHER   You don't want it?

MOTHER   What's the point when I'm dying?

FATHER   You believe the doctor?

MOTHER   I believe how I feel.

FATHER   Then it is serious? And all you think about is how it affects the children.

MOTHER   They're all that matters.

FATHER   Kristina, forgive me. For everything.

MOTHER   Oh yes? All right, forgive me too. We've both hurt each other. We don't know why. We couldn't help it. Look, here are the boys' new shirts. They have clean ones on Wednesdays and Sundays. And make sure Lina washes them all over. Are you going out?

FATHER   I have to be at college. It's nearly eleven.

MOTHER   Get Alfred for me first.

FATHER   But he's here already.

MOTHER   My eyes must be going. Or it's getting dark.

                She turns on the light.

                Alfred.

                FATHER *goes.*

                Who's that girl?

OFFICER   Agnes.

MOTHER   Oh is that Agnes? You know what they're saying? She's the daughter of the gods and she's come down to earth to find out what it's like to be a human being. But don't say anything.

                Alfred, before I die. Always remember this.

OFFICER	Yes.
MOTHER	Don't go on feeling life's been unfair to you.
OFFICER	But it has.
MOTHER	You were punished for stealing a coin that had just slipped down the back of the sofa.
OFFICER	Yes and it ruined my life.
MOTHER	Now go to the cupboard.
OFFICER	You know about that?
MOTHER	Treasure Island.
OFFICER	Don't.
MOTHER	Which your brother was punished for when it was you who tore it to pieces and hid it in the cupboard.
OFFICER	How can that cupboard be there after twenty years? We've moved house. And you died ten years ago.
MOTHER	So? You're always asking questions and ruining everything. Look, here's Lina.

LINA *enters.*

LINA	Thank you for giving me time off, ma'am, but I can't go anyway because I've nothing to wear.
MOTHER	Here, borrow this.
LINA	Oh ma'am, I couldn't.
MOTHER	Don't be silly. I won't be going out any more.
OFFICER	What will dad say? It was a present.
MOTHER	Alfred, that's so petty.

FATHER *pops his head round.*

FATHER	Are you lending my present to the maid?
MOTHER	Don't say maid like that, I was a maid once or have you forgotten? Why do you have to be so horrible to the poor girl?
FATHER	Why do you have to be so horrible to your husband?
MOTHER	Whenever you try to help someone you hurt someone else. I'm sick of life.

MOTHER *turns off the light.*

AGNES, OFFICER.

AGNES	I'm sorry for them.
OFFICER	Really?
AGNES	Yes, people find things so difficult. But there's always love. Look.

3. Outside the Stage Door

Enormous foxglove.

Green tree.

Fridge door.

Billboard.

AGNES, OFFICER, STAGE DOOR KEEPER, BILLSTICKER.

STAGE DOOR KEEPER *is sewing.*

AGNES	Is that the same star blanket you're still making?
SD KEEPER	Twenty-six years isn't long.

AGNES   And he never came back?

SD KEEPER   It wasn't his fault.

AGNES   (*To* BILLSTICKER.) Didn't she used to be a ballet dancer?

BILLSTICK   Yes, she was a prima ballerina. But when he left, her dancing went with him and she stopped getting the parts.

AGNES   Everyone's complaining. If it's not what they say, it's how they look.

BILLSTICK   I don't, not now I've got my fishing net and my bucket. That's what I wanted when I was four and now I'm fifty-four and I've got them.

AGNES   Fifty years for that.

BILLSTICK   It's a green bucket.

AGNES   (*To* SD KEEPER.) Lend me your coat and I'll sit here and watch.

She puts on the coat and sits down.

SD KEEPER   It's nearly the end of the season and today they hear if they're going to be kept on.

AGNES   And what if they're not?

SD KEEPER   I hide my face.

SINGER *crosses in tears.*

Look, she's been dropped.

AGNES   Poor things.

BILLSTICK   No, this one's happy. He's going to marry Victoria.

OFFICER *enters with bunch of roses.*

OFFICER	Victoria!
BILLSTICK	She'll be right down.
OFFICER	The taxi's here, I've booked a table, the champagne's on ice. I have to give you a hug.

He hugs STAGE DOOR KEEPER *and* AGNES.

Victoria!

VICTORIA	(*Off.*) Coming!
AGNES	Don't you know me?
OFFICER	Sorry, I only know Victoria. I've been walking up and down for seven years. You can see how my feet have worn a path. Ah she's mine. Victoria! (*He waits.*) She's getting dressed. I see you've got a fishing net. Everyone at the opera loves fish even though they can't sing. How much does a thing like that cost?
BILLSTICK	You have to save up.
OFFICER	Victoria! (*Of tree.*) Look, it's turning green again. Eighth time.

Victoria! She's combing her fringe. Excuse me, I have to go up and fetch my bride.

SD KEEPER	No one's allowed in the dressing rooms.
OFFICER	Seven times three hundred and sixty-five is . . . two thousand five hundred and fifty-five days. And I've looked at this door two thousand five hundred and fifty-five times without knowing where it goes. What is it? Does anyone live there?
SD KEEPER	I don't know. I've never seen it opened.

OFFICER   It looks like a fridge door I saw when I was
                 four and the maid took me out one Sunday
                 afternoon. Different families, different maids,
                 but I never got further than the kitchen and I
                 liked sitting under the table. I've seen so
                 many kitchens and the fridge doors were
                 always the same. But the opera can't have a
                 fridge because it hasn't got a kitchen.
                 Victoria! Listen, I don't suppose she could
                 come out a different way?

SD KEEPER   No, this is the only way out.

OFFICER   Good, then I can't miss her.

                 THEATRE PEOPLE *come out.*

                 She'll be here soon. I saw that identical
                 foxglove when I was seven in a vicarage
                 garden. There were two blue pigeons. Then
                 a bee flew into one of the bells and I thought
                 'got you' and grabbed the flower and the bee
                 stung me right through it and I cried. But
                 then the vicar's wife put wet earth on it and
                 we had wild strawberries and milk for supper.
                 It seems to be getting dark. (*To*
                 BILLSTICKER.) Where are you going?

BILLSTICK   Home to supper.

OFFICER   Evening? Now? Listen, can I use the phone?
                 I have to phone the tower.

AGNES   What for?

OFFICER   I want to tell the glazier to put in double-
                 glazing. It's nearly winter and I feel the cold.

                 OFFICER *goes.*

AGNES   Who is Victoria?

BILLSTICK   The one he loves.

AGNES	Yes, that's all he knows about her. He doesn't care about what she means to other people. Just what she is to him, that's all she is.

BILLSTICKER *goes.*

Suddenly it's dark.

SD KEEPER	Getting dark quickly today.
AGNES	A year can feel like a minute.
SD KEEPER	No, a minute can feel like a year.

OFFICER *comes back, dusty, roses withered.*

OFFICER	She hasn't come down yet.
SD KEEPER	No.
OFFICER	She will come. She will come. But maybe I'll cancel lunch. Yes, that's what I'll do.

He goes.

SD KEEPER	Can I have my coat now?
AGNES	No, you have a break and I'll stay here. I want to find out more about life.
SD KEEPER	You don't get any sleep in this job.
AGNES	Not at night?
SD KEEPER	You can have a doze if you don't mind being woken up, because the security guards change every three hours.
AGNES	What a horrible job.
SD KEEPER	Plenty of people want it.
AGNES	Want to be woken up?
SD KEEPER	That's not the worse thing, or the cold and the damp. It's hearing all their troubles. There's thirty years of trouble in that coat.

AGNES	It's heavy and scratchy.
SD KEEPER	Call me when it gets too much.
AGNES	Goodbye. If you can bear it, I can.
SD KEEPER	Be kind to them.

STAGE DOOR KEEPER *goes.*

The leaves have fallen from the tree, the foxglove has wilted. OFFICER *enters, his hair and beard are grey, his clothes worn and dirty. The roses are just stems.*

OFFICER   It seems to be autumn. I can tell by the tree. But autumn's spring for me because that's when the theatre opens for the new season. And then she'll come. Do you mind if I sit down for a moment?

AGNES   Please do. I can stand.

OFFICER   If only I could get some sleep it wouldn't be so bad.

I can't stop wondering about this door. What's behind it?

Faint music.

They've started rehearsals.

Alternate light and dark.

What's going on? Light dark, light dark.

AGNES   Day night, day night. So you don't have to wait so long.

BILLSTICKER *returns.*

OFFICER   Catch anything?

BILLSTICK   Yes, plenty. But the summer was a bit hot and rather long. It's a very good net but not quite what I imagined.

OFFICER	No, this isn't quite what I imagined.
BILLSTICK	She hasn't come?
OFFICER	Not yet, she'll be down in a minute. You don't happen to know what's behind this door?
BILLSTICK	No, I've never seen it open.
OFFICER	I'm going to phone a locksmith.

OFFICER *goes.*

AGNES	What was wrong with the net?
BILLSTICK	No, it's fine. But it wasn't quite what I imagined. I did enjoy it but . . .
AGNES	How did you imagine it?
BILLSTICK	It's hard to say.
AGNES	Maybe green but not exactly that green?
BILLSTICK	That's why everyone likes talking to you. Could you spare a few minutes?
AGNES	Come in here and tell me.

Tree green again and foxglove in bloom.

OFFICER *enters, old with white hair, worn shoes, carrying stems.*

BALLET DANCER *enters.*

OFFICER	Has Victoria left?
DANCER	No, not yet.
OFFICER	Then I'll wait. I expect she'll be down soon.
DANCER	I expect so.
OFFICER	Don't go, I've sent for the locksmith, you'll see what's behind this door.

DANCER   That's interesting. That and the tower that
               keeps growing. Do you know the tower?

OFFICER   I was a prisoner there.

DANCER   Really? were you?

               SINGER *enters.*

OFFICER   Has Victoria left?

SINGER   No, she never leaves.

OFFICER   That's because she loves me. Please don't go.
               There's a locksmith coming to open the door.

SINGER   Opening the door? what fun. There's just
               something I want to ask the stage-door
               keeper.

               PROMPTER *enters.*

OFFICER   Has Victoria left?

PROMPTER   Not as far as I know.

OFFICER   There, didn't I tell you she was waiting for
               me? Don't go, we're about to open the door.

PROMPTER   Which door?

OFFICER   Is there more than one door?

PROMPTER   Oh this one. Yes, I'll stay to see that. Just
               need to have a word with the stage-door
               keeper.

               GLAZIER *enters.*

OFFICER   Is that the locksmith?

GLAZIER   No, he had friends round, but a glazier's just
               as good.

OFFICER   Yes, of course. Did you bring your diamond?
               Let's do it.

More SINGERS *and* DANCERS *enter in opera costumes.*

Thank you all for coming. This is a once in a lifetime moment, so I ask you to –

Armed POLICEMEN *enter, shouting.*

POLICE   Keep away from the door.

OFFICER   Oh god, whenever you try to do something new. But we'll see them in court. A solicitor!

4. Room (Solicitor's Office)

AGNES, OFFICER, SOLICITOR.

SOLICITOR   Let me take your coat. I'll put it in the bin.

AGNES   Not yet. I know it's disgusting because it's full of people's problems but I want to get even more. I'd like to soak up all the crimes you know about and the false imprisonments and abuse.

SOLICITOR   Your coat's not big enough. The pain's spattered all over the room, it's stained the wallpaper.   It's all over me, my hands are black, look they're cracked and bleeding. I can only wear my clothes a couple of days and then they stink. I use air freshener but it's no good. I sleep here as well and all my dreams are violent. I'm in the middle of a murder trial now, but that's all right. Do you know what's worse? Divorce. When you think how they started out full of wonder and love, and they go on for pages and pages accusing each other and making themselves out to be right. And if someone just kindly and simply asked them what it's really all about they wouldn't know. They quarrelled about a green salad. They quarrelled about a word. They quarrelled about nothing. But the pain. Look at me. No woman's going to want me after all this. No one even wants to be friends with me.

AGNES   I'm so sorry.

SOLICITOR   You should be. And what do people live on? They don't earn enough to get married so they're always in debt. (*To* OFFICER.) What do you want?

OFFICER   I just wanted to ask if Victoria's left.

SOLICITOR   No, she definitely hasn't. Why are you pointing at my cupboard?

OFFICER   I thought the door looked like . . .

SOLICITOR   Oh no no no.

Bells.

OFFICER   Is it a funeral?

SOLICITOR   No, it's an honours ceremony. And I'm going to be given an honour. Would you like to be knighted for something or other?

OFFICER   Yes, why not. It's something to do.

Ceremony.

SOLICITOR *goes forward but is refused.*

AGNES *enters. The coat is clean.*

AGNES   Look how clean it is. But what's the matter? Didn't you get it?

SOLICITOR   I'm not good enough.

AGNES   Why? because you do legal aid? because you get people off? and if they're found guilty you get them shorter sentences. Some criminals do do terrible things of course but I'm still sorry for them.

SOLICITOR	Don't say anything against them. I'll always defend them.
AGNES	But why do they hurt each other?
SOLICITOR	They can't help it.
AGNES	Maybe we could make them better. Together.
SOLICITOR	No one's going to listen to us. If only the gods knew what it's like.
AGNES	They will, I promise. Do you know what I can see in this mirror? The world the right way round. Because usually it's the wrong way round.
SOLICITOR	How did it get the wrong way round?
AGNES	When it was copied.
SOLICITOR	Yes, I always thought there was something wrong with the copy. I sometimes think there's an original which was much better and then I feel really depressed. Everyone does. Like a glass splinter in your eye.
AGNES	Let me play for you.

She plays organ but we hear voices.

VOICES	Whoever's up there have mercy on us save us and spare us please don't be angry.

5. Cave

SOLICITOR, AGNES.

SOLICITOR	Where are we?
AGNES	What can you hear?

SOLICITOR	Drips. Drops.
AGNES	Tears. What else?
SOLICITOR	Sighs. Wailing.
AGNES	So why all this complaining? What's it about? Don't people enjoy anything?
SOLICITOR	Love. They do like love. A partner and a home.
AGNES	Can I try it?
SOLICITOR	With me?
AGNES	With you. You know all the mistakes we mustn't make.
SOLICITOR	I'm poor.
AGNES	That doesn't matter so long as we love each other. And beauty doesn't cost anything.
SOLICITOR	There are things I hate, and you might turn out to like them.
AGNES	Then we'll both have to change a bit.
SOLICITOR	And what if we get tired of each other?
AGNES	We'll have a baby.
SOLICITOR	Would you really have me? poor, ugly? a failure?
AGNES	Yes, let's share our lives.
SOLICITOR	Let's do that.

6. Room (One-Room Flat at Solicitor's)

AGNES, KRISTIN.

KRISTIN *is pasting the windows shut to keep out draughts.*

KRISTIN   Pasting, pasting.

AGNES   You're shutting out the air. I'm suffocating.

KRISTIN   There's just one little crack left.

AGNES   I can't breathe.

KRISTIN   Pasting, pasting.

                 SOLICITOR *enters.*

SOLICITOR   That's good, Kristin. It saves money on
                 heating.

AGNES   It's as if you're sticking my mouth together.

SOLICITOR   Is she asleep?

AGNES   At last.

SOLICITOR   All that screaming drives away the clients.

AGNES   What can we do?

SOLICITOR   Nothing.

AGNES   We need a bigger place.

SOLICITOR   We can't afford it.

AGNES   Do you mind if I open the window? I can't
                 breathe.

SOLICITOR   You'll let the heat out, it's too cold.

AGNES   I know, let's scrub the office so it looks better.

SOLICITOR   You haven't got the strength and nor have I,
                 and Kristin has to keep pasting, she's got to
                 paste the whole building tight, every crack in
                 the ceiling, the floor, the walls.

AGNES   I don't mind being poor. I just don't like dirt.

SOLICITOR   Being poor can lead to dirt.

AGNES   It's worse than the worst I imagined.

SOLICITOR   Things aren't too bad. We've plenty to eat.

AGNES   Lentils?

SOLICITOR   Lentils are good for you.

AGNES   I hate lentils.

SOLICITOR   Why didn't you say so?

AGNES   I was trying to put up with it because I love you.

SOLICITOR   Then I must give up lentils. We both have to change.

AGNES   What can we eat? Fish? You hate fish.

SOLICITOR   Fish is expensive.

AGNES   This is harder than I expected.

SOLICITOR   You see? And the baby, who should make us closer, just makes things worse.

AGNES   Beloved, I'm going to die in this air, in this room, looking down on the backyard, the baby screaming all night, no sleep, the neighbours shouting. I'm going to die.

SOLICITOR   Poor little flower. No light, no air.

AGNES   And you say there are people who are worse off.

SOLICITOR   I'm one of the lucky ones.

AGNES   I think I'd be all right if I had something beautiful.

SOLICITOR   I know you want flowers, you want that azalea you saw in the shop, but it costs as much as forty pounds of potatoes.

AGNES   I'd go without food if I could have a flower.

SOLICITOR   There is a kind of beauty you can have for
             nothing. And not having it really hurts if
             you're a man who loves beauty.

AGNES   What is it?

SOLICITOR   You'll be angry.

AGNES   We've agreed we'll never get angry.

SOLICITOR   Yes, we've agreed we can say anything to
             each other but not in that angry voice. Do
             you know what I mean? You've never heard
             it, have you?

AGNES   You'll never hear it from me.

SOLICITOR   And never from me.

AGNES   So say it.

SOLICITOR   Well, when I go into someone's house, the
             first thing I notice is how the curtains hang. If
             any of the hooks are missing, I walk out.
             Then I look at the chairs. If they're straight,
             I'll stay. Then I look at the lamps. If the
             shades are askew, the whole house is off-
             balance. And this is the beauty you can have
             for nothing.

AGNES   Not in that tone of voice.

SOLICITOR   It wasn't.

AGNES   Yes it was.

SOLICITOR   For god's sake.

AGNES   What did you say?

SOLICITOR   I'm sorry, Agnes. But I mind your untidiness
             just as much as you mind the dirt. And I
             didn't like to do any tidying up in case you
             thought I was criticising. Ugh. Shall we stop
             this?

AGNES   Marriage is really difficult, isn't it? You have
               to be an angel.

SOLICITOR   Yes, ideally.

AGNES   I might start hating you after this.

SOLICITOR   That would be horrible. But let's see it
               coming and not let it happen. I'll never say
               anything about untidiness again. Though I
               do hate it.

AGNES   And I'll eat lentil soup though I hate that.

SOLICITOR   So a life of what we hate. That's going to be
               fun.

AGNES   I'm really sorry for people.

SOLICITOR   You see?

AGNES   Yes but let's try to find a way through. We
               can see what the problems are.

SOLICITOR   Yes, we're intelligent enough to understand
               each other.

AGNES   If little things go wrong we can have a laugh.

SOLICITOR   Of course we can. I saw something this
               morning in the paper – where is the paper?

AGNES   What paper?

SOLICITOR   Do we get more than one paper?

AGNES   Laugh about it. And not that tone of voice. I
               used it to wrap up the potato peelings when I
               threw them away.

SOLICITOR   Oh for god's sake.

AGNES   Please smile. There was an article which
               made me really upset.

SOLICITOR   And which I agreed with. Well. I'll smile, I'll
               smile till you see my back teeth. I'll be nice

and not say what I think and agree to
everything and pretend. So you threw away
my paper. I see. Look, I'm tidying up again
which makes you angry. Agnes, this is
impossible.

AGNES   Yes, it is.

SOLICITOR   But we've got to stay together because of the
baby.

AGNES   You're right. For the baby. Oh. Oh. We've
got to stay together.

SOLICITOR   And now it's time to go and see some clients,
who are all desperate for me to keep them
out of prison and make someone else go
instead. They're beside themselves.

AGNES   Poor poor people. And the pasting.

KRISTIN   Pasting. Pasting.

SOLICITOR *is fiddling with the door.*

AGNES   Don't make the bolt squeak. It's as if you're
squeezing my heart.

SOLICITOR   Squeezing. Squeezing.

AGNES   Don't do it.

SOLICITOR   Squeezing.

AGNES   No.

SOLICITOR   Squeez –

OFFICER *enters and adjusts the bolt.*

OFFICER   Allow me.

SOLICITOR   Please. Since you've got a knighthood.

OFFICER   Yes, life's all before me. Fame and glory.

SOLICITOR   What will you live on?

OFFICER   Live on?

SOLICITOR   Don't you need a home? clothes? food?

OFFICER   That all sorts itself out so long as someone loves you.

SOLICITOR   I suppose so. I suppose so. Paste, Kristin. Paste till they can't breathe.

SOLICITOR *goes out.*

KRISTIN   Pasting. Pasting till they can't breathe.

OFFICER   Will you come away with me?

AGNES   Yes but where to?

OFFICER   The seaside. It's summer there. Sunshine, flowers, children −

AGNES   I want to go.

OFFICER   Come on.

SOLICITOR *comes back.*

SOLICITOR   Look, hairpins all over the floor again.

OFFICER   He's noticed the hairpins too.

SOLICITOR   As well as what? Look, two sides, one pin. Two and one. If I straighten it out, it's one. If I bend it it's two but it's still one. It means 'these two are one.' But if I snap it − then they're two, two.

OFFICER   To break it the prongs have to go apart. If they get closer, it holds.

SOLICITOR   And if they're parallel they never meet.

OFFICER   It's perfect and impossible. A straight line which is two parallels.

SOLICITOR	A bolt which locks when it's open. And when I close the door, I open a way out for you, Agnes.

SOLICITOR *goes.*

AGNES	So?

7. Quarantine Station by the Sea

Scorched earth.

Pigsties.

In the distance, on the other side of the bay, a beautiful seashore, villas, boats.

RICH FAT SICK *exercising on machines like instruments of torture.*

AGNES, OFFICER, QUARANTINE MASTER.

QUARANTINE MASTER *is wearing a monster mask.*

OFFICER	We're in the wrong place.
Q MASTER	Aren't you the one who's waiting outside the theatre?
OFFICER	Yes, I am.
Q MASTER	Have you got the door open yet?
OFFICER	No, we're still in the middle of the appeal. The billsticker's gone off with his net so it's taking a while to get all the evidence. But the glazier's put new windows in the tower and it's grown another ten floors. It's been a good year for growing, hot and wet.
Q MASTER	Not as hot as here.

OFFICER	How hot do you keep your furnaces then?
Q MASTER	Sixty centigrade to disinfect for cholera.
OFFICER	Cholera? is there cholera?
Q MASTER	Didn't you know?
OFFICER	Yes, I do know of course, but I forget about it.
Q MASTER	I wish I could forget. What I'd really like is to forget myself. That's why I go to parties.
OFFICER	Why, what's happened to you?
Q MASTER	If I talk about it they say I'm boasting and if I don't they say I'm a hypocrite.
OFFICER	Is that why you dress up as a monster?
Q MASTER	Yes, just a little more monstrous than I am.
OFFICER	Who's this?
Q MASTER	A writer with an appointment for a mud bath. It gives him a thick skin.

Enter WRITER.

WRITER	Lina.

LINA *enters.*

Lina, let Miss Agnes have a look at you. She knew you ten years ago when you were young, happy and even pretty. Look at her now. Five children, hunger, beatings. All that beauty destroyed by duty, which we're told produces inner tranquillity reflected in the −

Q MASTER	Shut up, shut up.
AGNES	Tell me what's wrong.
LINA	I'll get into trouble.
AGNES	Who's cruel to you?

LINA   I'll get a beating.

WRITER   That's what it's like, Agnes.

OFFICER   Visitors.

                HE *and* SHE *are passing in a boat.*

                Look, perfect happiness. Young love.

                HE *sings.*

HE   When I was a child
                I was lonely here.
                Same sea, same woods, same
                sky, same sun, but all
                new now with my love.

OFFICER   It's Victoria.

Q MASTER   What?

OFFICER   It's his Victoria. I still have my own.
                Raise the quarantine flag. I'll pull them in.

                QUARANTINE MASTER *waves a yellow flag.*

                OFFICER *tugs a rope, pulling the boat in.*

                Hold it.

                HE *and* SHE *react to quarantine station with
                disgust.*

Q MASTER   Yes yes, of course you don't like it. But all
                passengers arriving from infected areas have
                to land here.

WRITER   How can you do this to people in love? Don't
                touch them.

HE   What have we done wrong?

Q MASTER   Nothing. You can still have a bad time.

SHE   We'd only just started to be happy.

HE	How long do we have to wait?
Q MASTER	Six weeks.
SHE	Then we'd rather go home.
HE	We can't stay here. Scorched earth.
WRITER	Don't worry, you're in love. And that's even stronger than sulphur.
Q MASTER	I'm lighting the sulphur now. This way please.
SHE	My dress isn't colourfast.
Q MASTER	No, it's going to turn white. And so will the roses.
HE	So will your face. In six weeks.
SHE	(*To* OFFICER.) I suppose you're happy now.
OFFICER	No. Not really. Seeing you happy did make me feel a bit low but I've got a knighthood now so I've got that status, ha ha, oh yes. And this autumn I'll start teaching. Teaching boys what I learned all through my childhood. And now I'll teach it all my adult life and all my old age, the same stuff. What's twice two? How many times does two go into four? Till I get my pension and wander round with nothing to do, waiting for meals and newspapers till I'm taken off to the crematorium to be burnt. And Victoria, whom I loved and wanted to be happy, she is happy and that makes me miserable.
SHE	So how can I be happy? Perhaps you'll feel better while I'm a prisoner here. Does that help?
OFFICER	I can't be happy if you're miserable. Oh.

HE	And how can I be happy now I realise what I've done to you?
OFFICER	I'm sorry for all of us. Oh.
ALL THREE	Oh.
AGNES	Life's really difficult. I'm sorry for all of them.
ALL THREE	Oh.

8. Outside a Ballroom by the Sea

The quarantine station is in the distance on the other side of the bay.

MAIDS *are outside watching the dancing through a window.*

Ugly EDITH *is sitting outside.*

A piano.
A yellow house.
Children in summer clothes playing.
A jetty with boats and flags.
In the bay, a warship.
Bare trees and snow.

AGNES *and* OFFICER *enter.*

AGNES	This is the place we meant to come to. Every day's a holiday and parties start in the morning. (*To* MAIDS.) Why don't you go inside and dance?
MAIDS	Us?
OFFICER	They're the help.
AGNES	Oops. But why isn't Edith dancing?
	EDITH *hides face in hands.*

OFFICER   Don't ask. She's been sitting in there for
               three hours and nobody's asked her to dance.

               OFFICER *goes into the yellow house.*

AGNES   Parties are a cruel kind of fun.

               MOTHER *in party dress comes out of the
               ballroom.*

MOTHER   Why don't you come inside? I keep telling you.

EDITH   I know I'm ugly and no one wants to dance
               with me but I don't have to sit in there
               offering myself.

               EDITH *plays the piano – Bach Toccata con Fuga
               10. Music from ballroom rises to compete, then is
               drowned out by it.* GUESTS *come out of the
               ballroom and everyone listens to her playing.*

               Naval LIEUTENANT *seizes* ALICE, *one of the
               guests, and takes her off to the jetty.*

LIEUTENANT   Come on, quick.

               EDITH *stops playing.*

               In the yellow house.

               SCHOOLBOYS, OFFICER *sitting among
               them,* TEACHER.

TEACHER   Twice two.

               OFFICER *can't remember.*

               Stand up when I ask you a question.

OFFICER   Twice two. I think . . . It's two two.

TEACHER   So you didn't do your homework?

OFFICER   Yes I did. I do know it. I can't say it.

TEACHER   You know it but can't say it? Maybe I can
               help you. (*Pulls his hair.*)

OFFICER   This is terrible.

TEACHER   It's terrible that a big boy like you has no ambition.

OFFICER   A big boy, yes I am big, I'm bigger than the others. I'm grown up, I've finished school. I've got a knighthood. So why am I sitting here? Haven't I just been given a knighthood?

TEACHER   Yes but you have to sit here until you get a sense of responsibility.

OFFICER   Yes, you have to be responsible. Twice two . . . equals two and I can prove that by analogy. One times one is one. So two times two is two.

TEACHER   Logical but wrong.

OFFICER   Logic can't be wrong. Let's try again. One goes into one once. So two goes into two twice.

TEACHER   Then what's one times three?

OFFICER   Three.

TEACHER   And it follows logically that two times three is also three.

OFFICER   No, that can't be right . . . it can't be . . . or perhaps . . . No, I haven't got a sense of responsibility.

TEACHER   You certainly haven't.

OFFICER   So how long do I have to go on sitting here?

TEACHER   How long? Do you believe time and space exist? If time exists, you should be able to say what it is. What's time?

OFFICER	Time? I can't exactly say but I know what it is. So I can know what twice two is and not be able to say it. Can you tell me what time is?
TEACHER	Of course.
BOYS	Then say it.
TEACHER	Time flies while we speak. So time is something that flies while I'm speaking.
BOY	You're speaking now and I'm going to fly, so I'm time.

BOY *flies.*

TEACHER	That's certainly logical.
OFFICER	But it must be wrong because he can't be time.
TEACHER	That's logical.
OFFICER	So logically, logic must be wrong.
TEACHER	But if logic's wrong, everything's crazy and how can I teach it?
OFFICER	You can't, you're an old idiot.
TEACHER	Don't be impertinent.
OFFICER	I'm an officer, I'm an officer, and I don't see why I'm sitting here with schoolboys getting told off.
TEACHER	Where's your sense of responsibility?

QUARANTINE MASTER *enters.*

Q MASTER	The quarantine's beginning.
OFFICER	He's making me learn my tables and I've got a knighthood.

Q MASTER	So why don't you leave?
OFFICER	I can't.
TEACHER	I thought not. Try.
OFFICER	Save me. Save me from his eyes.
Q MASTER	Come on then. Come and help us dance. We must have a dance before the plague breaks out.
OFFICER	And after that the warship's going to sail?
Q MASTER	It's going to sail first. There'll be tears.
OFFICER	There's always tears. When it goes and when it comes back. Let's go.

They leave TEACHER *teaching.*

MAIDS *and* EDITH *go sadly to the jetty.*

AGNES, OFFICER, QUARANTINE MASTER.

AGNES	This is paradise. But isn't anyone happy here?
OFFICER	Yes, listen. They've just got married.

Enter NEWLYWEDS.

HUSBAND	I'm so happy I could die.
WIFE	Die? why?
HUSBAND	Because bliss burns out. And that means I can't bear it.
WIFE	Let's die together. Now.
HUSBAND	Die? Yes. Because I'm frightened of happiness.

They go.

AGNES	People are so fucked up.
OFFICER	Tell me about it.
	Now here's somebody everyone wants to be.
	Enter BLIND MAN.
	He owns a hundred villas, he owns the whole coast. All the beaches, forests, all the fish in the sea, birds in the air, animals in the woods. Thousands of people pay him rent and the sun rises over his waves and sets over his hills.
AGNES	And I suppose he thinks he's got something to complain about?
OFFICER	He does because he can't see.
Q MASTER	He's blind.
AGNES	The one they want to be.
OFFICER	He's come to wave goodbye to the warship, his son's on it.
BLIND MAN	I can't see but I can hear. I can hear the anchor tearing the seabed like when you tear a fishhook out of a fish and the heart comes out of its throat. My son's being sent overseas. I can't go with him except in my thoughts. The chains are squeaking . . . and something's fluttering . . . wet handkerchiefs . . . and there's sobbing and sniffing, but it could be the small waves against the nets . . . but it could be the girls on the beach, the girls they've left behind them. I once asked a child whose father was at sea why the sea was salt, and he said because sailors cry. Why do they cry? Because they're so far away. And they put their handkerchiefs on the masts to dry. So then I asked him why do people cry when

they're sad? And he said because they have to wash their eyes so they can see better.

Ship sails. GIRLS *waving sadly.*

Signal flag with red raised on the ship. ALICE *waves happily.*

AGNES   What does the flag mean?

OFFICER   It means yes. It's the lieutenant's yes in red, like blood on the sky's blue uniform.

AGNES   What's no?

OFFICER   Blue like the sick blood in his veins. See how happy Alice is.

AGNES   And how Edith's crying.

BLIND MAN   I met his mother and she left me. I still had my son and now he's gone too.

AGNES   But I'm sure he'll come back.

BLIND MAN   Who's that? I've heard that voice in my dreams. I used to hear it on the first day of the summer holidays. I heard it the first time I made love to my wife. I heard it the night my son was born. It's like a south wind. It's like angels.

SOLICITOR *enters and whispers to* BLIND MAN.

I see.

SOLICITOR   Yes, that's the sort of person she is.

Right, Agnes, you've seen a lot but you haven't tried the worst yet.

AGNES   What's that?

SOLICITOR   Repetition. Going back. Doing it all over again. Come on.

AGNES	Where?
SOLICITOR	To your duties.
AGNES	What duties?
SOLICITOR	Everything you always hated.
AGNES	The lentils and dirty clothes?
SOLICITOR	Yes, it's washday and we're washing the handkerchiefs.
AGNES	Do I have to do it all over again?
SOLICITOR	Life's all repetition. Look at the teacher. Right, let's go home.
AGNES	I'd rather be dead.
SOLICITOR	Yes but you're not allowed to kill yourself. It's against the law and you don't get a proper funeral and then you're damned.
AGNES	I'm finding it really hard being a person.
ALL	See.
AGNES	I'm not coming. I want to stay here. Compared to life with you, this is paradise.

Two BUILDING WORKERS.

BW1	This is hell.
BW2	Forty degrees in the shade.
BW1	Shall we go for a swim?
BW2	We'll be arrested. We can't swim here.
BW1	We could pick some fruit.
BW2	No, we'll be arrested.
BW1	I'm not working in this heat. I'm off.
BW2	You'll be arrested. And anyway you'll starve.

BW1	(*To* AGNES.) So, what do you think? What's your answer?
AGNES	I'm not sure yet. Is it true they're not allowed to swim here?
SOLICITOR	They can try to drown themselves. But then they get beaten up at the police station.
AGNES	Can't they go further down the coast and swim in the countryside?
SOLICITOR	It's all fenced off.
AGNES	No, I mean where it doesn't belong to anyone.
SOLICITOR	It all belongs to someone.
AGNES	But not the sea?
SOLICITOR	Everything. You can't moor a boat without being charged for it. Good, isn't it?
AGNES	Why don't people do something about it?
SOLICITOR	Some of them do but they end up in prison or a psychiatric ward.
AGNES	Who puts them in prison?
SOLICITOR	The great and the good, the law-abiding citizens and the hard-working families.
AGNES	Who puts them in the psychiatric ward?
SOLICITOR	Their own despair.
AGNES	Maybe it has to be like this.
SOLICITOR	That's exactly what some people think.
	GENTLEMAN *and* LADY *cross.*
LADY	Are you coming to play cards?
GENT	No, I need some exercise so I can eat dinner.

SOLICITOR   Please don't think I'm a socialist but does
             there have to be such a big difference?

AGNES   It isn't paradise.

SOLICITOR   So come back with me.

AGNES   No, I'm not going back to dirt and lentils and
             arguments. I want to go back where I came
             from. But first we've got to get the door
             open. I want them to open the door.

SOLICITOR   Then you have to go back the way you came
             and go through everything again.

AGNES   All right, if I have to. But first I'm going
             somewhere quiet where there's no people
             because I'm confused. I will see you later. (*To*
             WRITER.) Come with me.

9. Cave

AGNES, WRITER.

WRITER   Where have you brought me?

AGNES   Away from all that. To the edge of the world.
             To a cave where the gods listen to people's
             complaints.

WRITER   How? Here?

AGNES   Look, the cave's shaped like a shell. And an
             ear is shaped like a shell. You know how you
             can listen to a shell and hear the sound of
             your own blood and the thoughts in your
             brain? So if you can hear that in a small
             shell, imagine what you can hear in this big
             one.

WRITER   I can only hear the wind.

AGNES
I'll tell you what it's saying.
Over the cities
with their foul smoke and
over the sea to
wash our dusty feet
and shake out our wings.
People aren't evil
and people aren't good.
They live how they can
one day at a time.
They come out of dust
they go back to dust,
dusty feet, no wings,
and whose fault is that?

WRITER
I've heard this before.

AGNES
Sh. The winds are still singing.
Hear us in autumn
crying down chimneys
or moaning through the
cracks of windows, when
the rain's beating down.
Hear us in winter
in forests in the
snow, at sea hear us
in the ship's rigging.
We learnt to howl from
people, we heard them
in bed sick, on the
ground in a battle,
we heard their pain and
that's why we're wailing.

WRITER
I thought I . . .

AGNES
Sh. Now the waves are singing.
We rock the winds to
sleep, like wet flames we
burn quench make destroy,
rocking them to sleep.

Look what's been washed up from wrecked
ships. Rowlocks. Bailers. A lifejacket. And
part of a guided-missile launcher.

WRITER   Here's a nameboard. Enduring Freedom.
That's from the ship we saw sail with the
blind man's son. And the lieutenant Alice
and Edith loved.

AGNES   Didn't I dream all that? There was a blind
man and Alice and Edith. And the
quarantine and the sulphur and the honours
and the solicitor and Victoria and the tower
and the officer . . . I dreamt that.

WRITER   I wrote it.

AGNES   Then you know what poetry is.

WRITER   I know what a dream is. What's poetry?

AGNES   It's not real but maybe it's more than real.
It's dreaming while you're awake.

WRITER   Everyone thinks it's playing and nonsense.

AGNES   That's just as well or everyone would lie
about and you'd never even have invented
agriculture.

WRITER   It's easy for you to say. You don't belong
here, you belong in the sky.

AGNES   Yes, I've been here too long. I can't fly any
more. (*Raises her arms.*) I'm sinking. (*To gods.*)
Help me. (*Silence.*) I can't hear anything any
more. I've lost contact. I'm stuck here.

WRITER   Were you planning to . . . go up soon?

AGNES   I'll have to burn off the dust. It won't wash
off in the sea. Why?

WRITER   Because I have a sort of petition.

AGNES   What about?

WRITER   From all us people to god, the gods,
           whatever.

AGNES   And you want me to . . . ?

WRITER   Take it with you.

AGNES   Will you say it?

WRITER   Yes, all right.

AGNES   Say it then.

WRITER   I'd rather hear you say it.

AGNES   How can I read it?

WRITER   Read my mind.

AGNES   Yes, I'll say it.

> Why does it hurt to
> give birth? why do babies
> cry? why are we just
> animals and not gods?

Sh. No one understands what life is.

> We race over stones
> and thistles, if we pick
> flowers they're someone
> else's, if we're happy
> it makes someone sad,
> if we're sad it doesn't
> make them happier.
> And then we just die.
> This isn't a good tone to take with
> gods.

WRITER   How can I find words
           to tell them what it's like?
           Put it your own way.

AGNES   Yes, I'll try.

WRITER   What's floating over there? Is it a buoy to
               warn the ships?

AGNES   Yes, it sings when there's danger.

WRITER   I think the sea's rising now. I can hear
               the waves thundering. And what's that?
               A ship . . . on the rocks. Shouldn't the buoy
               be making some sort of noise? Look, the
               sea's rising. We're going to be trapped in the
               cave. That's the ship's siren. It's going to be
               wrecked. The buoy –

               Buoy sound.

               The crew's waving to us. But we're going to
               die too.

AGNES   Don't you want to be released from this
               terrible life?

WRITER   Yes of course but not now. Not in the water.

               CREW *on ship singing*

CREW   Christ our Lord.

WRITER   No one can hear them.

AGNES   Who's that out there?

WRITER   Walking on the water? There's only one
               person who's ever done that.

CREW   Christ our Lord?

AGNES   Is that him?

WRITER   It is, it is, it's the one who was crucified.

AGNES   Why was he crucified?

WRITER   Because he wanted to set people free, I think.

AGNES   Who wanted to crucify him?

WRITER   The great and the good, the law-abiding
                citizens and the hard-working families.

AGNES   This world is so odd.

WRITER   The sea's rising. It's dark. The storm's getting
                up.

                CREW *scream.*

                And the crew are screaming with terror.
                They've seen him walking on the water to
                save them and they're so terrified they're
                jumping overboard. Now they're screaming
                because they're going to die.

                Waves threaten to drown AGNES *and* WRITER
                in the cave.

AGNES   If I could be sure it was a ship . . .

WRITER   You know . . . I don't think it is a ship. It's a
                house with trees outside . . . and a telephone
                tower . . . a tower that goes right up into the
                sky. A tower with wires to take messages to
                the gods.

AGNES   They don't need wires.

WRITER   No, it's not a house, not a telephone tower,
                can you see it?

AGNES   What do you see?

WRITER   It's a plain covered with snow. It's the army's
                training ground. The sun's shining behind a
                church and the spire's shadow's on the snow.
                Here come the soldiers. They're marching on
                the church, marching up the spire, I think the
                one who steps on the weathercock's going to
                die. They're getting nearer. The corporal's
                leading them. Haha. Here comes the shadow
                of a cloud rushing across, blots it all out, the
                steeple's shadow's gone.

10. Outside the Stage Door

AGNES, OFFICER, STAGE DOOR KEEPER.

AGNES   Have the great and the good arrived yet?

SD KEEPER   Not yet.

AGNES   Then call them at once because we've got to
               open the door. Everyone thinks the meaning
               of life is in there.

               STAGE DOOR KEEPER *blows whistle.*

               And don't forget the glazier with his
               diamond.

               THEATRE PEOPLE *enter.*

               OFFICER *enters with roses, as at the beginning.*

OFFICER   Victoria!

SD KEEPER   She'll be right down.

OFFICER   That's good. The taxi's waiting, I've booked
               a table, the champagne's on ice. I have to
               give you a hug. (*He hugs* STAGE DOOR
               KEEPER.) Victoria!

VICTORIA   (*Off.*) Coming.

OFFICER   Good. I'll wait.

WRITER   You know that feeling that something's
               happened before.

AGNES   Yes, me too.

WRITER   Maybe I dreamt it.

AGNES   Or wrote it?

WRITER   Or wrote it.

AGNES   Then you know what poetry is.

WRITER   I know what a dream is.

AGNES   I think we've said this before too.

WRITER   You'll soon be able to work out what reality is.

AGNES   Or dreaming.

WRITER   Or poetry.

              Enter CHAIRMAN OF INQUIRY, BISHOP, PSYCHOANALYST, SCIENTIST *and* BARRISTER.

CHAIR   I am here to chair an inquiry into the opening of the door. What do you think, bishop?

BISHOP   I don't think, I believe, and I believe the door should not be opened because it conceals a dangerous truth.

PSYCH   The patient fears the truth. And the analyst helps him live with it. In an ordinary unhappy way.

SCIENTIST   What is 'the truth'? Forty-six chromosomes. Thirty thousand genes.

BARRISTER   It's what I can prove beyond a reasonable doubt.

PSYCH   Truth is what you discover about yourself after years of lying on the couch.

SCIENTIST   That's not scientific truth. It's talk.

              BISHOP *cheers.*

PSYCH   What are you cheering for? you hate science. You think the world was made in six days ten thousand years ago.

SCIENTIST *cheers.*

BISHOP   What are you cheering for? You only know
                what's under your microscope. Our truth is
                always true and yours constantly changes.

SCIENTIST   Idiot.

                Fight.

CHAIR   The truth is outside the terms of reference of
                this inquiry. Perhaps we should move to the
                opening of the door.

BISHOP   I am the way, the truth and the light.

PSYCH   The Oedipus complex.

SCIENTIST   The prefrontal cortex.

BARRISTER   Prove it, prove it, prove it.

ALL   (*Cheer.*) The door's open.

CHAIR   What's behind the door?

GLAZIER   I can't see anything.

CHAIR   No, he might not perhaps be capable.
                Bishop, what's behind the door?

BISHOP   Nothing. That's the answer. God created
                everything out of nothing.

PSYCH   The feeling of nothingness can be a
                symptom of –

SCIENTIST   There's simply nothing there.

OFFICER   Nothing there?

BARRISTER   I doubt that. This is a case of conspiracy to
                deceive. I appeal to the great and the good,
                the law-abiding citizens and the hard-
                working families.

ALL   We've been deceived.

CHAIR	Who has deceived you?
ALL	She has.
CHAIR	What did you mean by opening the door?
AGNES	If I told you, you wouldn't believe me.
SCIENTIST	The simple fact is there's nothing there.
AGNES	Nothing at all. But you don't understand it.
SCIENTIST	What is there to understand? It's a load of bollocks.
ALL	Bollocks. Get her.
BARRISTER	I grant you a conditional discharge provided you leave the country. You can go back where you came from. With what you got out of it.
AGNES	(*To* WRITER.) I'm sorry for them.
WRITER	Are you serious?
AGNES	Always serious.
WRITER	Sorry for the hard-working families, the law-abiding citizens and the great and the good?
AGNES	Them most of all. But what did he mean, what I got out of it?
WRITER	Don't worry about it. He was just talking.
AGNES	What I got out of coming to earth? I'm hurt by that.
WRITER	That's why he said it.
AGNES	Yes but –
ALL	She refuses to answer.
CHAIR	Get her.
AGNES	I've already answered.
ALL	She thinks she knows the answer, get her.

AGNES	Come on and I'll – a long way away – I'll tell you the secret where no one can see us or hear us. Because –

SOLICITOR *enters.*

SOLICITOR	Have you forgotten your duties?
AGNES	No. But I have higher duties.
SOLICITOR	And your daughter?
AGNES	My daughter. Anything else?
SOLICITOR	She's crying for you.
AGNES	This pain, what is it?
SOLICITOR	Don't you know?
AGNES	No.
SOLICITOR	Conscience.
AGNES	Conscience?
SOLICITOR	Yes and you'll get it every time you hurt someone else.
AGNES	Isn't there a cure?
SOLICITOR	Do your duty.
AGNES	What if I've got two duties?
SOLICITOR	Do one first, then the other.
AGNES	The highest first. So you look after our daughter, and I'll do my duty.
SOLICITOR	She misses you. Don't you understand? someone is suffering because of you.
AGNES	Now I'm torn in two.
SOLICITOR	This is one of life's little troubles, you see?
AGNES	It hurts.

WRITER	If you knew what grief I'd caused, you wouldn't want to hold my hand.
AGNES	Why? what?
WRITER	I did what I felt was my duty to my vocation and completely fucked up everyone who loved me. I gave my father a heart attack, my mother a nervous breakdown and stopped seeing my best friend because he was exploiting the people I was writing for. And it's no help thinking you did the right thing because next minute you think you were wrong. That's what life's like.
AGNES	Come with me.
SOLICITOR	You have a child.
AGNES	Goodbye.

11. Outside the Tower

Like the first scene, except the flowers are now bluebells. A chrysanthemum bud on top of the tower is about to open.

AGNES *and* WRITER.

AGNES	Soon I'm going up out of this world. I'll use fire. It's what you call dying and you're frightened of it.
WRITER	It's fear of the unknown.
AGNES	But you do know. Have you always doubted everything?
WRITER	No, sometimes I'm certain of something. Then it goes again. Like a dream when you wake up.
AGNES	It's not easy being alive.
WRITER	You know that now?

AGNES	Yes, I do now.
WRITER	But weren't you going to tell me the answer to whatever the question is.
AGNES	What's the point? You don't believe what you're told.
WRITER	I will believe you because I know who you are.
AGNES	All right, listen. (*Whispers.*)
WRITER	My dream.
	AGNES *whispers.*
	And then ?
	AGNES *whispers.*
	What about peace? and rest?
AGNES	Don't ask any more. I can't say any more. Because everything's ready for my death. Flowers. Candles. White sheets over the windows. And the fire.
WRITER	Why are you so calm? Are you someone who can't feel pain?
AGNES	I've felt yours. I've felt everyone's.
WRITER	Tell me what you've felt.
AGNES	Could you tell me? Could words ever do it?
WRITER	No, words are useless. I've always known what I write doesn't say what I mean so when I get praised I feel ashamed.
AGNES	Look into my eyes.
WRITER	I can't bear it.
AGNES	Then how would you bear my words if I spoke my own language?
WRITER	But tell me before you go. What was the worst thing about being down here?

AGNES   Just existing. Knowing my sight was blurred by my eyes, my hearing dulled by my ears, and my bright thought trapped in the grey maze of a brain. Have you seen a brain?

WRITER   And you're telling me that's what's wrong with us? How else can we be?

AGNES   First I'll get rid of the dust on my feet.

Puts shoes on fire.

Others enter, put things on fire, go.

SD KEEPER Do you mind if I burn my coat?

OFFICER My roses. Well, thorns, really.

BILLSTICK The posters can go but not my net.

GLAZIER The diamond which opened the door. Goodbye.

SOLICITOR My great lawsuit about asbestos poisoning.

Q MASTER A small contribution, my monster mask.

VICTORIA My beauty, my sadness.

EDITH   My ugliness, my sadness.

BLIND MAN My hands were my eyes.

WRITER   Sometimes when you're about to die, isn't your whole life meant to go past you in a flash? Is this it?

AGNES   It is for me. Goodbye.

WRITER   What about last words?

AGNES   I can't. Emotions don't fit into words.

KRISTIN *enters.*

KRISTIN   Pasting, pasting, till there's nothing left to paste.

WRITER   And if heaven cracked open you'd paste it
                shut. Go away.

KRISTIN   Aren't there some windows for me in the
                tower?

WRITER   No, Kristin.

KRISTIN   Then I'll go.

                KRISTIN *goes.*

AGNES   Goodbye, this is the
                end, goodbye writer,
                you live well floating
                in the air, plunging
                into the mud but
                not getting stuck there.

                When you're leaving you
                love what you've lost and
                you're sorry for what
                you've done and far more
                what you didn't do.
                I know what it's like.
                You want to stay and
                you want to go and

                Goodbye. Tell people
                I won't forget them.
                I'll tell the gods
                what being alive is.
                Because I'm sorry.
                Goodbye.

                She goes into the tower.

                The tower burns.

                The bud bursts into a giant chrysanthemum.

                End.

August Strindberg

Born in Stockholm in 1849, Strindberg studied medicine at the University of Uppsala, but soon turned to writing plays. As assistant librarian at the Royal Library, his personal affairs – and his creativity as a writer – took on an intensity which persisted throughout his life. As novels – *The Red Room, Son of a Servant* – and plays – *Master Olof, The Father, Comrades* – poured out of him, he fell in love with the first of a succession of women, many of them actresses. Siri von Essen divorced her husband to marry Strindberg in 1877 and had three children by him. As their marriage deteriorated, she probably provided the inspiration for *Miss Julie*, which premiered in Copenhagen in 1889, only to be closed down by the Danish censor.

In 1890 *The Father* was staged in Berlin, where Strindberg had settled after divorcing Siri. There he met Frida Uhl, marrying her in 1893 but almost immediately falling out with her. Returning to Sweden, he began work on the autobiographical *Inferno*, and in 1898 completed the first part of what was to become his dramatic trilogy, *To Damascus*. He met his third wife, the Norwegian actress Harriet Bosse, in 1900: in the spate of creativity that followed, he wrote *Easter, The Dance of Death* and *A Dream Play* (written in 1901, published in 1902), and then divorced her. Many of his plays remained unstaged until the early 1900s. The first public performance in Sweden of *Miss Julie* came in 1906. It was directed by August Falck, with whom Strindberg set up the experimental Intimate Theatre. He quickly created a repertoire of 'chamber' plays for the new theatre: *The Storm, After the Fire, The Ghost Sonata* and *The Pelican*. None met with much success, and when *The Great Highway* flopped badly, a row with Falck ended with the closure of the theatre in December 1910.

Strindberg died of stomach cancer in 1912. Earlier that year, his birthday had been marked by a torchlight procession through Stockholm – his radical journalism had earned him the title of 'people's writer'.

DRUNK ENOUGH TO SAY I LOVE YOU?

Drunk Enough to Say I Love You? was first performed at the Royal
Court Theatre Downstairs, London, on 10 November 2006,
with the following cast:

SAM   Ty Burrell
JACK   Stephen Dillane

Director James Macdonald
Designer Eugene Lee
Costume Designer Joan Wadge
Lighting Designer Peter Mumford
Sound Designer Ian Dickinson
Composer Matthew Herbert

The play received its American premiere at The Public Theater,
New York, on 5 March 2008, directed by James Macdonald,
and performed by Scott Cohen as Jack and Samuel West as
Guy.

Note

Sam was always called Sam, because of Uncle Sam. I gave the
other character the name Jack, thinking of it as just a name,
but some people understandably thought it referred to Union
Jack, and that Jack was Britain in the same way that Sam was
America. But I always meant that character to be an individual,
a man who falls in love with America, so I have changed his
name to Guy.

Caryl Churchill

Characters

SAM, *a country*

GUY, *a man*

1.

GUY	drunk enough to say I love you?
SAM	never say
GUY	not that I don't still love my wife and children but
SAM	who doesn't want to be loved? but
GUY	first time I saw you
SAM	the bar and the guy with
GUY	never see you again and I was fine with that, I thought one night and I'll love him till I die but that's ok, I can live
SAM	you know something?
GUY	and then I'm here and suddenly here you are and here we are again and
SAM	because I'm leaving tomorrow so
GUY	sorry of course but just as well because
SAM	and you could come with me if you
GUY	I
SAM	if you want
GUY	of course I
SAM	so you'll
GUY	so no I can't possibly
SAM	of course not

GUY   no

SAM   glad you came over and said hi because when
               you reminded me it all came back though to
               be honest I'd forgotten till you

GUY   can't say no oh god can't let you

SAM   so you'll

GUY   what I'm going to tell them. How long

SAM   as long as it

GUY   family obviously but work, I'm in the middle

SAM   sure you'll figure it out, I don't need to

GUY   go where did you say you?

SAM   anywhere you wouldn't?

GUY   do when we get there?

SAM   things you won't do?

2.

GUY	music, I can't get enough of
SAM	country or
GUY	when I listen to Bessie Smith or
SAM	Dylan, Bing Crosby, Eminem
GUY	because what rock does
SAM	even Jingle Bells can suddenly
GUY	the snow and all the
SAM	mountains like you've never
GUY	size of it all, there's so many different
SAM	sea to shining
GUY	freedom to
SAM	Ellis Island
GUY	or even just go to the movies and eat popcorn
SAM	pursuit of happiness
GUY	right now
SAM	how to keep
GUY	because it's so
SAM	elections
GUY	how to win
SAM	because democracy
GUY	help the right side to

SAM   because our security

GUY   all over the world

SAM   Vietnam we have the slogan 'Christ has gone
                   south' so the people think

GUY   Christians because of the French

SAM   literally believe literally Jesus Christ has

GUY   so clever

SAM   and simultaneously astrology

GUY   superstitious

SAM   horoscopes daily horoscopes will say

GUY   and they vote the way you want, that is so

SAM   because you have to appeal to their deepest

GUY   I love this

SAM   and Chile, this is good, we put it on the radio
                   'your children taken from you', if they vote
                   communist they lose their children, the
                   Russians will take

GUY   appealing to the women's vote

SAM   so the pamphlets must say 'privately printed
                   by citizens with no political affiliations'
                   because

GUY   big budget

SAM   and syndicate the articles all over the world

GUY   so nobody

SAM   and posters

GUY   great artwork

SAM   with the hammer and sickle stamped on their
                   foreheads

GUY   little kids

SAM   hammer and sickle

GUY   love a copy of that to put

SAM   So help me out here, in Nicaragua we need
             to be telling different things to different
             groups, say

GUY   fighting to keep the Russians off their land
             because peasants

SAM   while the workers

GUY   that they'll lose their factories

SAM   doctors

GUY   replaced by Cubans

SAM   way to go.

GUY   so happy, you, the work, the whole

SAM   polls in the Phillipines?

GUY   so I'll make the numbers up

SAM   good at this

GUY   thrilling.

SAM   don't always work out the way we

GUY   voting for the wrong

SAM   Chavez

GUY   how did

SAM   Hamas

GUY   Israelis arresting the Members of Parliament
             so

SAM   so now we need to prevent some elections

GUY	saves having to overthrow
SAM	South Korea, Guatemala, Brazil, Congo, Indonesia, Greece
GUY	I'm on it
SAM	overthrow only as last resort when things don't
GUY	ok
SAM	Iran Guatemala Iraq Congo
GUY	troops
SAM	coffee
GUY	two sugars
SAM	invading Grenada to get rid of the government because
GUY	byebye Lumumba
SAM	byebye Allende
GUY	bit negative
SAM	people we love and help
GUY	Israel
SAM	shah of Iran, byebye Mossadegh
GUY	oil
SAM	Saddam Hussein
GUY	great
SAM	shake his hand
GUY	holding down the ayatollahs
SAM	warlords in Afghanistan, Hekmatya

GUY   drives over people?

SAM   acid

GUY   ok

SAM   don't like that government in Afghanistan
               because the Russians like it so we're tricking
               them into invading

GUY   oops

SAM   puts them in the wrong plus it's their
               Vietnam so now get on with training the
               mujahadeen which is freedom fighters to

GUY   whooo

SAM   haha

GUY   so we're helping all these

SAM   kind of want to help Pol Pot because

GUY   killing fields guy?

SAM   against Vietnam but no we can't be seen to
               directly support someone who

GUY   so why don't we help China help him

SAM   knew I was right to bring you

GUY   because no one can blame us for what the
               Chinese

SAM   and all costs money

GUY   so much aid

SAM   and two hundred and fifty million dollars to
               the Phillipines alone to train fifty thousand
               soldiers

GUY   plus military advisers

SAM	remember to use Green Berets of Puerto Rican and Mexican descent so it won't look like a US army because
GUY	ha
SAM	would you believe six billion dollars in El Salvador? training thousands of
GUY	and the schools, I'm trying to organise
SAM	School of the Americas
GUY	coup school
SAM	Chemical School
GUY	enormous.
SAM	results in and we won in
GUY	yay
SAM	and we've got our man in Afghanistan
GUY	CIA guy?
SAM	Georgia check
GUY	Uzbekistan? because they boil
SAM	not so good in Bolivia
GUY	guy in the sweater?
SAM	and Saddam's let us down, he's no longer a good guy so
GUY	because sometimes propaganda isn't enough to
SAM	military solution
GUY	so much fun in my life
SAM	being powerful and being on the side of good is

GUY   God must have so much fun

SAM   win win win

GUY   love you more than I can

3.

SAM	sitting around
GUY	not
SAM	so much to do because
GUY	thinking
SAM	no time for
GUY	all right I'm just
SAM	missing your
GUY	not at all
SAM	natural
GUY	get on with
SAM	because there's all these people we have to
GUY	ok so here's the bridge right here and the people there are people going across not soldiers just
SAM	North Korea
GUY	blow it up
SAM	there you go
GUY	don't want you to worry because I don't regret
SAM	death squads
GUY	right behind

SAM	in Guatemala, so we don't directly ourselves appear to
GUY	corpses in the nets
SAM	decapitated, castrated, eyes gouged out, testicles
GUY	riddled with bullets and partially eaten by fish
SAM	slaughter the Indians to prevent
GUY	bulldoze the village
SAM	yes
GUY	and
SAM	not officially active in El Salvador
GUY	seventy-five thousand civilian
SAM	raping the
GUY	because if the young aren't killed they just grow up to be
SAM	similarly Colombia where
GUY	Nicaragua
SAM	our freedom fighters the Contras are
GUY	Indonesia the embassy's giving lists to their army which are a big help in who they should
SAM	mass slaying
GUY	there you are
SAM	and of course Israel where we don't actually ourselves
GUY	extremely valuable experiment in the Philippines where

SAM   calling it search and destroy

GUY   experiments in pacification

SAM   terror against the Huks

GUY   and applying that now in Vietnam

SAM   Vietnam Vietnam now

GUY   go go go three million dead in Vietnam Laos
               Cambodia

SAM   two million tons of bombs on Laos now

GUY   more than on Germany and Japan in the
               whole

SAM   white phosphorous

GUY   statistics here on civilian injuries, lower
               extremities 60%, soft tissue 39%, fractures

SAM   not that interested

GUY   Iraq

SAM   not that interested in numbers of civilian

GUY   no

SAM   need to get on

GUY   I'm on it

SAM   Iraq

GUY   hundred and seventy-seven million pounds of

SAM   forty days

GUY   ten thousand sorties

SAM   very few casualties

GUY   oh ours, good

SAM	bombing them now as they retreat
GUY	ploughing wow ploughing live soldiers into the sand
SAM	done
GUY	and the children dead from sanctions we don't count that because
SAM	again Iraq Iraq again
GUY	very few casualties
SAM	not publishing pictures
GUY	and certainly not of the civilians in Afghanistan there's a paper in Florida making a mistake there getting a lot of emails and won't do that again
SAM	bombing Vietnam now, bombing Grenada, bombing Korea, bombing Laos, bombing Guatemala, bombing Cuba, bombing El Salvador, bombing Iraq, bombing Somalia, bombing Lebanon
GUY	but it's Israel bombing
SAM	so? bombing Bosnia, bombing Cambodia, bombing Libya, bombing
GUY	used to be a village and now
SAM	because we want it gone
GUY	need a coffee
SAM	get a coffee
GUY	exhausting
SAM	thrilling
GUY	exhausting being so thrilled

SAM   coffee but keep

GUY   bombing China, bombing Panama

SAM   good at this

GUY   well

SAM   did a whole lot before like second world war
                and going right back

GUY   all the back killings before like Indians

SAM   never sure how many we started

GUY   maybe twenty million, fifty

SAM   got them down to a quarter million so

GUY   not looking at that

SAM   no just get on with the job which is bombing

GUY   bombing Peru, bombing

4.

GUY	controlling
SAM	not
GUY	I feel
SAM	missing your family
GUY	only human, I'm naturally going to
SAM	just so I know where I am
GUY	expect me to just cut off everybody and not even speak
SAM	what you want
GUY	better if I do some
SAM	drawing up trade agreements
GUY	free trade
SAM	in a manner of
GUY	free
SAM	Structural Adjustment Programs
GUY	so that countries open up their markets to our
SAM	good ok like Haiti
GUY	surge in our rice exports to Haiti
SAM	ok
GUY	stopping the banana cartel

SAM   ok

GUY   and those beautiful African textiles made
               from our raw materials they agree to import
               rather than

SAM   or sometimes it's the other way, it's their raw
               materials like cocoa

GUY   and we make the chocolates you get on
               Valentine's

SAM   because if they were allowed to make them

GUY   and the rice industry collapses in Haiti

SAM   because our economy is the priority here

GUY   costing poor countries two billion dollars a

SAM   really snitty mood today

GUY   just trying to understand exactly

SAM   essential because we consume more than half
               the goods in the world so you can't

GUY   ok ok and privatisation a condition

SAM   because private means free

GUY   ok

SAM   problem with that?

GUY   just low today, I can't quite

SAM   better get a grip

GUY   ok so it's access for our goods

SAM   come on we've done debt cancellation here

GUY   yes I

SAM   and massive aid

GUY	linked to
SAM	what is the matter with you?
GUY	pointing out that it's 80% our own companies that benefit from
SAM	generosity
GUY	point one percent of our
SAM	billions of dollars for christsake
GUY	just trying to see
SAM	yes and
GUY	Israel seems to get the largest share of
SAM	you want to go home?
GUY	didn't say
SAM	because if you don't want to be
GUY	I do
SAM	keep saying you love me and then we have all this
GUY	sorry
SAM	easy to
GUY	woke up feeling
SAM	maybe you should go back to bed and try again
GUY	no I'll be
SAM	you better be
GUY	ok.
SAM	something to make you feel better

GUY   don't really

SAM   good?

GUY   ah

SAM   french connection

GUY   mm?

SAM   golden triangle

GUY   sure

SAM   fighting Communists for us so we turn a
             blind eye

GUY   of course

SAM   heroin being flown in by Air America

GUY   excellent

SAM   flying down with the weapons and back with
             the drugs

GUY   shrimp company laundering the money so
             the CIA

SAM   22 tons of cocaine though he himself is head
             of the antidrug

GUY   but also we are against

SAM   totally

GUY   like in Peru

SAM   supporting the dictator because he's fighting
             drugs

GUY   though I see here the CIA payroll

SAM   because the main priority is suppressing the
             guerrillas

GUY   like in Colombia

SAM   because FARC are definitely narcotraffickers

GUY   luckily

SAM   have to overlook the security services drug

GUY   and the equipment can also be used against
               trade unionists which saves

SAM   but in Afghanistan where of course the
               mujahadeen

GUY   beautiful fields of poppies

SAM   same trucks can deliver the arms and take
               the heroin back

GUY   so sometimes crack down and

SAM   massive trade figures

GUY   lot of people happy.

SAM   feeling better have a look at intellectual
               property rights

GUY   fascinating

SAM   forefront of science

GUY   traditional knowledge of primitive tribes
               which turns out to

SAM   neem

GUY   is what, neem?

SAM   in India

GUY   so we patent it do we and

SAM   ayehuasca, you ever heard ?

GUY   quinoa, kava, bitter gourd

SAM	so we're manufacturing products out of
GUY	and selling them back to
SAM	yes
GUY	and most amazingly DNA
SAM	Amazonian Indian blood cells
GUY	the scale of it
SAM	per cent of human DNA has been acquired by
GUY	my god how
SAM	so you're on that?
GUY	I'm on it.
SAM	because expenses are so huge like eight billion dollars we spend on cosmetics
GUY	hard to grasp such
SAM	ten on petfood
GUY	for comparison
SAM	six on
GUY	enough to provide health, food and education for the whole of the third
SAM	fuck is wrong with you?
GUY	trying to grasp the numbers that's all, I
SAM	do things on a large scale
GUY	yes
SAM	way of life
GUY	yes

SAM	you chose
GUY	yes
SAM	can fuck off now if
GUY	no
SAM	yes fuck off now because
GUY	no please no
SAM	commitment

5.

SAM	space
GUY	god
SAM	all mine
GUY	so
SAM	deny others the use of space
GUY	it's just
SAM	we have it, we like it and we're going to keep it
GUY	fantastic
SAM	fight *in* space, we're going to fight *from* space, we're going to fight *into*
GUY	wow
SAM	you like it?
GUY	so big
SAM	star wars
GUY	and protect
SAM	protecting us with a shield
GUY	and nobody else can
SAM	precision strikes
GUY	though the UN
SAM	everyone else agrees a resolution not to use space so

GUY	giving us total
SAM	because with the proliferation of WMD
GUY	so many countries want
SAM	so we combat the threat by
GUY	I do worry about
SAM	because we have two and a half times the next nine countries put together
GUY	thank god
SAM	nuclear weapons stored in seven European
GUY	hey
SAM	chemical
GUY	whoo
SAM	go go go now dioxin
GUY	dioxin, god, three ounces in the water supply of New York would be enough to wipe out the whole
SAM	five hundred pounds dioxin now on Vietnam
GUY	yay
SAM	napalm
GUY	yay
SAM	sarin on Laos
GUY	yay
SAM	and biological too the most advanced
GUY	scientific
SAM	turkey feathers

GUY   feathers?

SAM   allegations by China that we

GUY   oh with germs on

SAM   decaying fish, anthrax

GUY   isn't it turkey in Cuba?

SAM   turkey virus in Cuba

GUY   ok

SAM   contaminate the sugar

GUY   quite funny

SAM   but the serious science

GUY   the Chemical School in Alabama

SAM   teach our allies and share

GUY   Egypt's using gas against the Yemen, and
               Saddam's gassing the

SAM   exporting anthrax to Iraq, botulism,
               histoplasma capsulatum

GUY   e coli?

SAM   e coli, DNA

GUY   this stuff against Kurds or Iranians or?

SAM   keep selling it because

GUY   so great about chemical and biological they
               don't destroy the buildings just kill the

SAM   ideal

GUY   and oh my god the conventional

SAM   cluster bombs

GUY	love the yellow
SAM	jagged steel shrapnel
GUY	soft targets
SAM	don't always explode like one and a half million unexploded in the gulf
GUY	very high rate of
SAM	no, out of thirty
GUY	ok
SAM	but sometimes a quarter
GUY	orange groves, car parks
SAM	so don't let Israel
GUY	ok
SAM	oh what the hell
GUY	ok
SAM	so you get these accidental
GUY	kids like the yellow
SAM	accidental loss of limbs
GUY	can't be helped
SAM	and the depleted uranium so you get the lung and bone cancer and
GUY	don't feel bad
SAM	babies, deformed
GUY	ugh
SAM	probably for other reasons
GUY	exactly

SAM   So, keeping ourselves safe

GUY   priority

SAM   bring freedom

GUY   love it when you say

SAM   most destructive power ever in the history of
               the

GUY   yes yes

SAM   and now space

GUY   stars

SAM   eternity filled with our

GUY   love you so

SAM   more and more

6.

SAM	faster
GUY	I'm
SAM	threat to our security
GUY	ok
SAM	if anyone harbours
GUY	I'm on it
SAM	retaliate against the facilities of the host country
GUY	yes
SAM	now
GUY	calm
SAM	got to plant bombs in the hotels in Havana
GUY	yes ok ok the Cuban exiles in Miami are just
SAM	and get the money to Iraq
GUY	done it, the Iraqi National Accord have the
SAM	and have they destabilised Saddam yet? no
GUY	car bombs
SAM	giving them millions
GUY	hundred civilians dead
SAM	not enough to
GUY	ok

SAM   fucking results

GUY   off my back will you?

SAM   desperate for

GUY   mujahadeen

SAM   yes yes train the

GUY   so ok that's something really good

SAM   stop at nothing, flaying, explosions, whole
               villages

GUY   and here we're getting on with assassinations

SAM   don't allow

GUY   changing our

SAM   do allow

GUY   ok

SAM   so get on with

GUY   CIA's Health Alteration Committee

SAM   great

GUY   planning

SAM   Castro, Allende, Ayatollah Khomeini

GUY   Lumumba, Osama, Charles de Gaulle

SAM   Michael Manley

GUY   Ngo Din Diem

SAM   but not all the bastards are dead so

GUY   disappeared, thousands and

SAM   all over the

GUY   impact

SAM	and what what fucking terror used against us
GUY	not my fault they
SAM	fucking Afghanis turned against us after all we
GUY	training camps and now
SAM	stop them
GUY	I'm
SAM	and Israel, innocent
GUY	body parts
SAM	vile
GUY	but the Israelis killing far more so
SAM	on top of this?
GUY	explosion at the embassy
SAM	fuck fuck do something
GUY	stop shouting at me because
SAM	on my side?
GUY	of course but
SAM	want to go home to your
GUY	maybe I do if you're going to keep
SAM	fuck off then back
GUY	look out we're being
SAM	no no no the towers
GUY	wow
SAM	evil
GUY	ok?

SAM   hate me because I'm so good

GUY   all these terrorists suddenly

SAM   makes everyone love me because it's only the
                 evildoers who hate me, you don't hate me

GUY   no of course

SAM   you hate me

GUY   just sometimes wish you'd

SAM   what? what? you hate me

GUY   but maybe I can't live with you any more

7.

SAM *alone.*

SAM   white double cable whip, iron wreath,
beating the soles of the feet, put object in
vagina, put object in anus, put turpentine on
testicles, pour water over face, play very loud
Indonesian music, electric shocks to genitals,
tap a dowl through the ear into the brain,
throw the prisoner out of the helicopter,
show the prisoner another prisoner being
thrown out of the helicopter, beating
obviously, rape of course, bright light, no
sleep, simulate an execution so they think up
to the last second they're going to die, play
tape of women and children screaming in
next room and tell prisoner it's his wife and
children, sometimes it is, hang up with hands
tied behind back, pins in eyes, insecticide in
hood over the head, cut off breasts, pull out
heart, slit throat and pull tongue through,
sulphuric acid, chop off

Enter GUY.

GUY   hello, I've

SAM   what you

GUY   but I missed you

SAM   same as before

GUY   try and

SAM   what you put me through

GUY   I'm sorry I

SAM   hurt me

GUY   yes I

SAM   take you back I need to know if

GUY   try to

SAM   total commitment or there's no

GUY   I realise

SAM   capable

GUY   can

SAM   promise

GUY   love

SAM   nightmare here

GUY   yes

SAM   not going to be happy, hope you don't

GUY   no I don't expect

SAM   so what you

GUY   can't live

SAM   no you can't, can't

GUY   no I can't

SAM   ok then

GUY   doing?

SAM   need to teach

GUY   yes

SAM   special advisers

GUY	ok
SAM	Greece
GUY	the colonels' Greece, we're right behind
SAM	Operation Phoenix
GUY	Vietnam, operational
SAM	nobody questioned survives
GUY	forty-one thousand
SAM	teaching them in Brazil exactly how much electric shock you can administer without killing
GUY	because sometimes you may not want
SAM	sometimes it's not politic
GUY	and sometimes it just doesn't matter
SAM	El Salvador, Uraguay, Nicaragua, Guatemala,
GUY	delivering the manuals to Panama
SAM	and the thin wire can go in the diplomatic bag to Uraguay
GUY	thin wire?
SAM	against the gum and it increases the shock
GUY	need to be accurate
SAM	precise pain
GUY	for precise effect
SAM	so practice on beggars in a soundproof room
GUY	the US Office of Public Safety
SAM	fighting terror

GUY	put Mitrione in charge of
SAM	humanitarian
GUY	expert in administration of pain
SAM	always leave them some hope, he says
GUY	people who don't need our encouragement because they already
SAM	Afghanistan
GUY	yes the game where the men are on horses and the prisoner
SAM	instead of a goat
GUY	one layer of skin at a time, which must take
SAM	so relatively speaking, Guantanamo
GUY	need results
SAM	need exemption from rules forbidding cruel, inhuman or degrading
GUY	because those rules
SAM	in the present climate
GUY	hoods over their heads or sexual
SAM	because their religion makes them upset by
GUY	menstrual blood
SAM	have to laugh
GUY	but some things we'd rather other people
SAM	747 rendering prisoners to
GUY	because there's plenty of places where that can
SAM	can't do everything ourselves

GUY   do our best

SAM   you're doing great again

GUY   back with you

SAM   no fun though

GUY   sick today but

SAM   just stick with it and we'll be

8.

GUY	icecaps
SAM	who fucking cares about
GUY	floods
SAM	because we'll all be dead by the time it
GUY	another hurricane moving towards
SAM	natural
GUY	no but it's greater than
SAM	natural disasters
GUY	not coping very
SAM	surprise
GUY	predicted and there is an element of manmade
SAM	stop fucking going on about
GUY	carbon
SAM	junk science.
GUY	report here from the
SAM	rewrites
GUY	'serious threat to health'
SAM	delete
GUY	'growing risk of adverse'

SAM	delete
GUY	'uncertainties'
SAM	insert 'significant and fundamental'
GUY	but
SAM	'urgent action,' delete
GUY	oil lobby?
SAM	Committee for a Constructive Tomorrow
GUY	ok
SAM	Advancement of Sound Science Coalition
GUY	a grassroots
SAM	set up by Exxon and Philip Morris to
GUY	ok
SAM	and carbon dioxide in the atmosphere has many beneficial effects on
GUY	hot in here?
SAM	always finding something wrong with
GUY	and you never?
SAM	let's just
GUY	ok
SAM	what? what? you smoking? you gave up, you
GUY	don't care because
SAM	kill yourself
GUY	fucking planet
SAM	kill me, kill me, secondhand
GUY	junk science

SAM   put it out

GUY   no

SAM   put it out

GUY   what difference

SAM   thank you

GUY   carbon

SAM   can't see it in the air, so

GUY   Kyoto?

SAM   price of electricity in California

GUY   but

SAM   nuclear

GUY   waste

SAM   solution

GUY   Iran?

SAM   Technology Institute will come up with new

GUY   by when will they

SAM   if you're so smart

GUY   different

SAM   freedom to

GUY   if

SAM   lose everything we've

GUY   hard to

SAM   things I need

GUY   look out

SAM	what?
GUY	don't know, I thought
SAM	deep breaths and
GUY	don't want to stop flying
SAM	trade in carbon so we can still
GUY	we'll last longer than
SAM	don't let them in
GUY	no water
SAM	be ok
GUY	catastrophe
SAM	so fucking negative
GUY	frightened
SAM	leave me if you don't
GUY	done that
SAM	stay then and be some
GUY	hopeless
SAM	and try to smile
GUY	dead
SAM	because you have to love me
GUY	can't
SAM	love me love me, you have to love me, you

End.